Windows PowerShell 4.0 for .NET Developers

A fast-paced PowerShell guide, enabling you to efficiently administer and maintain your development environment

Sherif Talaat

[PACKT] enterprise
PUBLISHING
professional expertise distilled

BIRMINGHAM - MUMBAI

Windows PowerShell 4.0 for .NET Developers

First published: January 2014

Production Reference: 1080114

Published by Packt Publishing Ltd.

Livery Place
35 Livery Street
Birmingham B3 2PB, UK.

ISBN 978-1-84968-876-5

www.packtpub.com

Cover Image by Suresh Mogre (suresh.mogre.99@gmail.com)

Credits

Author
Sherif Talaat

Reviewers
Mark Andrews
Mahmoud El-bagoury
Hosam Kamel
Shay Levy

Acquisition Editor
Vinay Argekar

Lead Technical Editor
Deepika Singh

Technical Editors
Iram Malik
Veena Pagare

Copy Editors
Janbal Dharmaraj
Sayanee Mukherjee
Alfida Paiva

Project Coordinator
Ankita Goenka

Proofreader
Lawrence A. Herman

Indexer
Tejal Soni

Production Coordinator
Sushma Redkar

Cover Work
Sushma Redkar

About the Author

Sherif Talaat is a young Computer Science addict. He holds many technology certificates. Sherif is working in the ICT industry since 2005; he used to work on Microsoft's core infrastructure platforms and solutions, with more focus on IT process automation and scripting techniques.

Sherif is one of the early adopters of Windows PowerShell in the Middle East and Africa. He speaks about Windows PowerShell at technical events and user groups' gatherings. He is the founder of *Egypt PowerShell User Group* (`http://egpsug.org`) and the author of the first and only Arabic PowerShell blog (`http://arabianpowershell.wordpress.com`). He has been awarded the Microsoft **Most Valuable Professional** (**MVP**) for PowerShell five times in a row since 2009.

You may also catch him at `sheriftalaat.com` and follow him on Twitter `@SherifTalaat`.

He is also the author of *PowerShell 3.0: Advanced Administration Handbook, Packt Publishing*.

Acknowledgments

I would like to take this chance to dedicate this book to the soul of my dad and to thank my mom for her love, encouragement, and prayers.

To Israa, the best wife and friend in the world, thanks for your love, support, and patience during the long days and nights I have spent writing this book. I could not have done this without you.

To my dear son Yahia, your little smile gives me the strength and power to do something that will make you proud of your dad. Keep it up, my son, this smile brightens up my life.

To my old friend Refaat Issa and my friends in Redmond from the PowerShell team, Dan Harman, Hemant Mahawar, and Indhu Sivaramakrishnan, thanks for your feedback, comments, and advice during the preparation phase. It helped me a lot in building strong content for this book.

To my mentor, Prof. Ahmed Bahaa, a special thanks for the time and effort you invested in helping me write the tremendous chapter for ALM and TFS.

To Shay Levy, having you as a reviewer was enough to make me feel comfortable while writing this book. Your comments and feedback have a great impact on the quality of the content.

Last but not least, thank you, Packt Publishing, for giving me the opportunity to work with you again. I'd also like to thank every team member who contributed to this project. To the external reviewers and the other guys whom I didn't meet—your contribution is invaluable, and this book wouldn't be what it is without you.

About the Reviewers

Mark Andrews' career in technology has been a varied one. Over the last 18 years, he has held several different positions ranging from customer service to quality assurance. In all of these positions, the responsibility for configuration management and build management has always fallen on Mark either personally or through one of the groups that he managed. Because of his "keeping a hand in" management style, he has been involved closely with the scripting and automation framework for this area. Creating scripted frameworks that intercommunicate across machines, operating systems, or domain boundaries is a passion for him.

Mahmoud El-bagoury is a Senior Web/Cloud Computing Developer. He is an MCSD and MCTS. He has been working in the ICT industry since 2005. He used to work with Ford Motors, US and Compuware, US as an Azure Cloud Solution Developer and Architect with the main focus on Azure deployment and automation process, Azure Cloud security, and developing SmartCloud-based web apps (SaaS).

He is one of the early adopters of Windows Azure in the Middle East and Africa. Also, he is among the rare developers in the world who use open source Apache SolrCloud solutions for Big Data search engine with Azure PaaS and Microsoft PowerSell.

Hosam Kamel is currently a Regional Technology Solution Professional working for MEA Center Of Expertise, specializing in Visual Studio **Application Lifecycle Management** (**ALM**) and Team Foundation Server. His main focus is helping software professionals and organizations build better applications and solutions using Microsoft Application Lifecycle Management technologies, practices, and tools. He works with development teams and helps them eliminate traditional silos between development, testing, and project management to establish cohesive processes with the Visual Studio ALM tools. His experience with Team Foundation Server and Visual Studio started with the beginning of the VSTS and its product family, nearly seven years ago.

He is also an active Visual Studio ALM Ranger with contributions to many projects. He has also authored several articles and spoken at various user groups, events, and conferences. You can find him sharing his experience on his technical blog at `http://blogs.msdn.com/hkamel` and on Twitter with his handler `@HosamKamel`.

Shay Levy works as a Systems Engineer for a government institute in Israel. He has over 20 years' experience, focusing on Microsoft server platforms, especially on Exchange and Active Directory.

He is a worldwide-known, knowledgeable figure in the PowerShell scripting arena, and is very active on forums and user-group sessions. He is a **Microsoft Certified Trainer** (**MCT**) at the John Bryce training center, and for his contribution to the community he has been awarded the Microsoft **Most Valuable Professional** (**MVP**) award for six years in a row.

He is the co-founder and the editor of the `PowerShellMagazine.com` website, and as a long time PowerShell community supporter he also moderates multiple PowerShell forums, including the official Microsoft PowerShell forum and The Official Scripting Guys Forum on Microsoft TechNet.

He often covers PowerShell related topics on his blog at `http://PowerShay.com`, and you can follow him on Twitter at `http://twitter.com/ShayLevy`.

Shay was also the technical reviewer of the best-selling PowerShell book, *Microsoft Exchange 2010 PowerShell Cookbook* by *Mike Pfeiffer*, *Packt Publishing*.

www.PacktPub.com

Support files, eBooks, discount offers and more

You might want to visit www.PacktPub.com for support files and downloads related to your book.

Did you know that Packt offers eBook versions of every book published, with PDF and ePub files available? You can upgrade to the eBook version at www.PacktPub.com and as a print book customer, you are entitled to a discount on the eBook copy. Get in touch with us at service@packtpub.com for more details.

At www.PacktPub.com, you can also read a collection of free technical articles, sign up for a range of free newsletters and receive exclusive discounts and offers on Packt books and eBooks.

PACKTLIB™

http://PacktLib.PacktPub.com

Do you need instant solutions to your IT questions? PacktLib is Packt's online digital book library. Here, you can access, read and search across Packt's entire library of books.

Why Subscribe?

- Fully searchable across every book published by Packt
- Copy and paste, print and bookmark content
- On demand and accessible via web browser.

Free Access for Packt account holders

If you have an account with Packt at www.PacktPub.com, you can use this to access PacktLib today and view nine entirely free books. Simply use your login credentials for immediate access.

Instant Updates on New Packt Books

Get notified! Find out when new books are published by following @PacktEnterprise on Twitter, or the *Packt Enterprise* Facebook page.

Table of Contents

Preface

Windows PowerShell has been proven to be a strong automation tool that has various usages for IT professionals as well as developers. This object-based scripting language became part of many Microsoft servers and development tools. The enhanced .NET integration along with the new web cmdlets in Windows PowerShell 4.0 made it a developer-friendly tool.

Windows PowerShell 4.0 for .NET Developers comes with a set of easy-to-follow practical examples and real-world scenarios that will help you in getting started with PowerShell, understanding the syntax and grammar, building your scripts and modules, and integrating them with different technologies and tools.

This guide starts with the essential topics of PowerShell along with new features in PowerShell 4.0, then goes through building scripts and modules, and then goes deep into integration topics. Next, it covers PowerShell integration with .NET, WMI, and COM.

Moreover, we will use PowerShell to manage Windows Server, Internet Information Services, SQL Server, and Team Foundation Server. Finally, we will be working with XML and RESTful web services.

What this book covers

Chapter 1, Getting Started with Windows PowerShell, introduces us to Windows PowerShell and the new features in Version 4.0. It also introduces us to the difference between PowerShell, other command-line tools, and programming languages. Also, it covers the syntax fundamentals and grammar of the language.

Chapter 2, Unleashing Your Development Skills with PowerShell, demonstrates both simple and advanced examples of how to make use of PowerShell integration with technologies such as .NET, WMI, CIM, and COM. It also covers extending Windows PowerShell's capabilities for writing scripts and building modules.

Chapter 3, PowerShell for Your Daily Administration Tasks, focuses on using Windows PowerShell with different technologies and tools that you might use on a daily basis, such as Windows Server, SQL Server, and Internet Information Services.

Chapter 4, PowerShell and Web Technologies, focuses on unveiling the hidden power of PowerShell cmdlets to work with web technologies, including but not limited to web services, RESTful applications, and social networking.

Chapter 5, PowerShell and Team Foundation Server, provides instructions on how to use PowerShell to work with Visual Studio Team Foundation Server for more productive and effortless automated application lifecycle management.

What you need for this book

This book requires you to have Windows PowerShell 4.0, which is available out of the box in Windows Server 2012 R2 and Windows 8.1. It is also available for earlier versions of Windows as a part of Microsoft **Windows Management Framework (WMF)** Version 4.0.

This book is mainly about using Windows PowerShell with different technologies and tools, so you must have the following software in order to proceed:

- Windows Server 2012 R2
- SQL Server 2012
- Visual Studio 2012/2013
- Visual Studio Team Foundation Server 2012/2013

Who this book is for

This book is intended for the .NET developers who are willing to learn Windows PowerShell and want to quickly come up on discovering Windows PowerShell and its capabilities with different tools and technologies.

Conventions

In this book, you will find a number of styles of text that distinguish between different kinds of information. Here are some examples of these styles, and an explanation of their meaning.

Code words in text, database table names, folder names, filenames, file extensions, pathnames, dummy URLs, user input, and Twitter handles are shown as follows: "You can get this path within your PowerShell by using a predefined variable called `$PSHome`."

A block of code is set as follows:

```
Function Reload-Module($ModuleName)
{
if((get-module -list | where{$_.name -eq "$ModuleName"} | measure-
object).count -gt 0)
{
  if((get-module -all | where{$_.Name -eq "$ModuleName"} | measure-
object).count -gt 0)
  {
    Remove-Module $ModuleName
    Write-Host "Module $ModuleName Unloading"
  }
  Import-Module $ModuleName
  Write-Host "Module $ModuleName Loaded"
}
Else
{
  Write-Host "Module $ModuleName Doesn't Exist"
}
}
```

Any command-line input or output is written as follows:

```
PS C:\> Get-CimInstance -Query $Query | Select DeviceID, Name
DeviceID              Name
--------              ----
0                     Intel(R) 82579LM Gigabit Network Connection
2                     Intel(R) Centrino(R) Ultimate-N 6300 AGN
```

New terms and **important words** are shown in bold. Words that you see on the screen, in menus or dialog boxes for example, appear in the text like this: "clicking the **Next** button moves you to the next screen."

[Warnings or important notes appear in a box like this.]

[Tips and tricks appear like this.]

Reader feedback

Feedback from our readers is always welcome. Let us know what you think about this book—what you liked or may have disliked. Reader feedback is important for us to develop titles that you really get the most out of.

To send us general feedback, simply send an e-mail to `feedback@packtpub.com`, and mention the book title via the subject of your message.

If there is a topic that you have expertise in and you are interested in either writing or contributing to a book, see our author guide on `www.packtpub.com/authors`.

Customer support

Now that you are the proud owner of a Packt book, we have a number of things to help you to get the most from your purchase.

Downloading the example code

You can download the example code files for all Packt books you have purchased from your account at `http://www.packtpub.com`. If you purchased this book elsewhere, you can visit `http://www.packtpub.com/support` and register to have the files e-mailed directly to you.

Errata

Although we have taken every care to ensure the accuracy of our content, mistakes do happen. If you find a mistake in one of our books—maybe a mistake in the text or the code—we would be grateful if you would report this to us. By doing so, you can save other readers from frustration and help us improve subsequent versions of this book. If you find any errata, please report them by visiting `http://www.packtpub.com/submit-errata`, selecting your book, clicking on the **errata submission form** link, and entering the details of your errata. Once your errata are verified, your submission will be accepted and the errata will be uploaded on our website, or added to any list of existing errata, under the Errata section of that title. Any existing errata can be viewed by selecting your title from `http://www.packtpub.com/support`.

Piracy

Piracy of copyright material on the Internet is an ongoing problem across all media. At Packt, we take the protection of our copyright and licenses very seriously. If you come across any illegal copies of our works, in any form, on the Internet, please provide us with the location address or website name immediately so that we can pursue a remedy.

Please contact us at `copyright@packtpub.com` with a link to the suspected pirated material.

We appreciate your help in protecting our authors, and our ability to bring you valuable content.

Questions

You can contact us at `questions@packtpub.com` if you are having a problem with any aspect of the book, and we will do our best to address it.

1
Getting Started with Windows PowerShell

When Microsoft introduced the .NET framework many years ago, a new powerful environment for development was introduced, giving no limits for developers' innovation to build applications and create solutions that fit nearly all needs. One major key for the success of .NET is its powerful library that keeps growing over different versions. Also, it provides an ease of use for such a library, taking away all the freaky processes of managing database connections, controlling a socket, formatting UI controls, and many more routines that developers encounter in everyday life in their work.

Moreover, another great tool was introduced as well that can have a major impact on speeding up and smooth management of the created solutions; yes, it is the Windows PowerShell. Built itself on the .NET Framework, PowerShell provides the super flexibility of a scripting language that gives a middle ground between developers and IT professionals, getting them near each other and providing a simple, easy-to-learn language for automating and managing common tasks.

In this chapter, we will cover the following topics:

- Windows PowerShell—the story behind it
- Windows PowerShell features under the spot
- Windows PowerShell fundamentals
- Windows PowerShell syntax and grammar

Introducing Windows PowerShell

Windows PowerShell has been proven to be a strong automation tool that has various usages for IT professionals as well as developers; that is why you might hear different answers for this question: What is Windows PowerShell? One of the answers is "it is a scripting language"; other answers are, "it is a command-line interface", "it is an automation tool", and others. The good news is that there is no wrong definition for Windows PowerShell; each person defines it according to his own use of it. So the optimum and widest definition for Windows PowerShell is that it is an automation engine that provides a task-based command-line interface, a dynamic scripting environment, an interactive shell engine, and much more. All of these are bundled together in one component and shipped with the Windows operating system in order to provide a common automation platform for Microsoft technologies, alongside interoperability and integration with various technologies from different vendors.

Windows PowerShell is also available as part of **Windows Management Framework** (**WMF**). The WMF is a package that includes updates and enhancements to different management technologies such as PowerShell, **Windows Remote Management** (**WinRM**), and **Windows Management Instrumentation** (**WMI**). The WMF allows to use the latest management technologies on older operating systems. For example, WMF 4.0 allows you to use Windows PowerShell 4.0 on Windows Server 2008 R2 with SP1 or Windows 7 with SP1.

Windows PowerShell has been built on top of .NET framework, **Common Language Runtime** (**CLR**), and **Dynamic Language Runtime** (**DLR**). This architecture made it a powerful, dynamic, consistent, and extensible shell. Also it made PowerShell an object-based (object-oriented) shell where everything is produced as an object (.NET object) unlike other shells that deal with everything as raw text. Using the .NET framework makes the Windows PowerShell syntax almost like C# except for some differences in specific areas. Also, it made it easy to deal with other technologies such as **Component Object Model** (**COM**), **Windows Management Instrumentation** (**WMI**), and **Extensible Markup Language** (**XML**).

Moreover, it is possible to compile C# code inside PowerShell and execute PowerShell code as part of the code managed by .NET. Last but not least, PowerShell is shipped with its own **Application Programming Interface** (**API**) to give you the capability to build customized PowerShell commands and extensions for your own developed applications.

Windows PowerShell became part of Microsoft's **Common Engineering Criteria** (**CEC**) program in 2009. In case you don't know what the Microsoft CEC is, it is a program started in 2005 to define, unify, and standardize a set of engineering requirements across all Microsoft server products; some of these requirements are related to security, automation, and manageability. In other words, starting with 2005, each Microsoft server product must follow and pass these requirements before being released to the end users. In our case, starting with 2009, each and every server products must provide a management interface via Windows PowerShell. Today, almost all Microsoft server products support Windows PowerShell.

> Read more about Microsoft CEC at `http://www.microsoft.com/cec/en/us/default.aspx`.

In Windows PowerShell, we refer to commands as cmdlets (pronounced "command-lets") where each cmdlet represent a function or task-based script. The cmdlets can be used individually for simple tasks or together in combination to perform more complex tasks. A cmdlet has a consistent naming style known as verb-noun, where each cmdlet has a verb and a noun separated by a dash (-) symbol, for example, `Get-Service`, `Restart-Computer`, and `Add-User`. This naming style makes the cmdlets' names easier to remember and even to guess and expect the new cmdlets. Windows Server 2012 is shipped with more than 2,400 cmdlets covering most of Windows Server roles and features.

Windows PowerShell consoles

Windows PowerShell has multiple consoles: Windows PowerShell console and Windows PowerShell **Integrated Scripting Environment** (**ISE**), which had been introduced with Version 2.0. On 64-bit operating systems, you will find two instances of each: a 32-bit instance and a 64-bit one.

> The `PowerShell.exe` and `PowerShell_ISE.exe` files are located at the following path: `%WINDIR% | System32 | WindowsPowerShell | v1.0`. **You can get this path within your PowerShell by using a predefined variable called** `$PSHome`.

The two consoles provide (almost) the same capabilities in terms of core usage of Windows PowerShell, same cmdlets, same modules, and even the same way of execution; however, the Windows PowerShell ISE provides more features in terms of usability and user experience. The following couple of paragraphs will describe the differences between both the consoles.

The Windows PowerShell console

The Windows PowerShell console is the basic console for Windows PowerShell and it is very similar to the command prompt console (`cmd.exe`). From the end user perspective, both almost look the same for the first time except that the Windows PowerShell console host has a blue background and the command prompt has a black background. However, the core functionality is totally different. The console host is a good choice for on-the-fly (interactive) usage of PowerShell such as executing inline cmdlets, scripts, or native win32 commands.

The following screenshot illustrates the look of the Windows PowerShell console host:

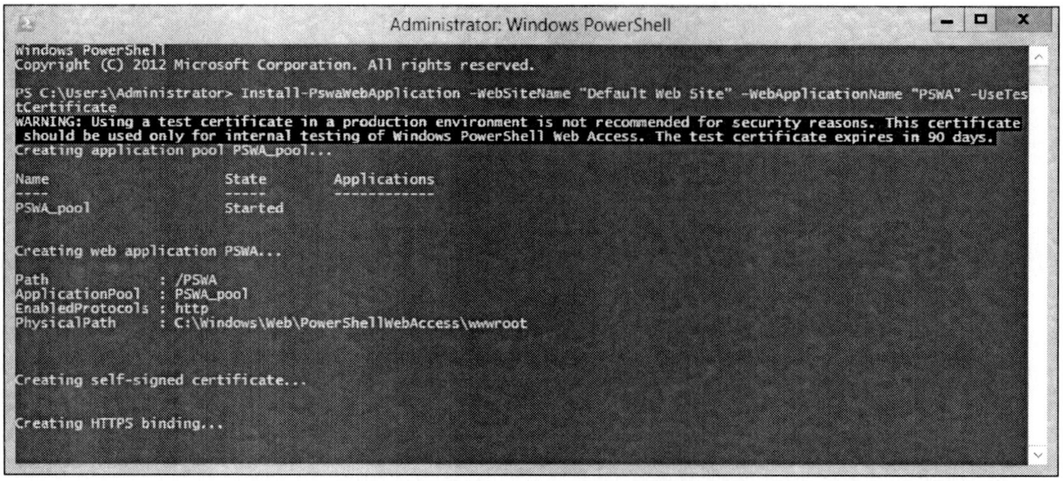

The Integrated Scripting Environment (ISE)

Windows PowerShell ISE is the **Graphical User Interface** (**GUI**) editor for Windows PowerShell, and it is similar to the PowerShell console host but with more advanced features. The ISE is similar to the **Integrated Development Environment** (**IDE**), such as Microsoft Visual Studio.

The following screenshot illustrates the Windows PowerShell ISE:

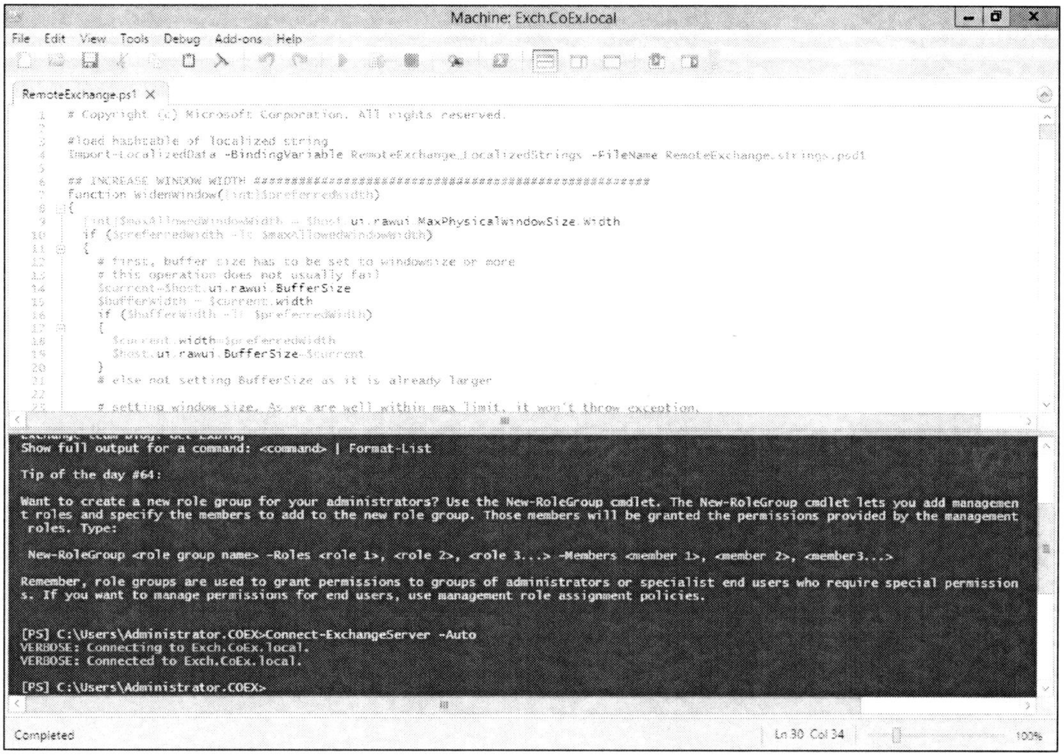

You can think of the Windows PowerShell ISE as a mini scripting IDE. You can also see that Windows PowerShell ISE shares a lot of features with Visual Studio, such as:

- Syntax highlighting and coloring for PowerShell and XML
- Script snippets (also known as code snippets)
- Script debugging, code parsing, and error indicators
- Brace matching and code regions
- Support for remote script debugging
- Support for Windows PowerShell Workflow debugging
- Console customization such as font sizes, zoom, and colors
- Multiple tabs (local and remote) to work simultaneously on several independent tasks
- Full unicode support, execute, edit, and display complex scripts and right-to-left languages
- IntelliSense support for Windows PowerShell syntax, Desired State Configuration providers, and configurations

In addition to the features adapted from Visual Studio, Windows PowerShell has its brand new unique features, such as:

- **Modules Auto-Loading and cmdlets discovery**: PowerShell automatically loads and discovers all PowerShell modules available in your system. Thus, you do not have to know which module is needed for which cmdlet. Simply, Windows PowerShell will take care of discovering all modules and finding which modules are required for your script to be executed and then loading them if they were not loaded before.
- **Add-on tools**: Add-on tools are **Windows Presentation Foundation** (**WPF**) controls that can be added to the PowerShell ISE to add extra features and functionalities, such as spelling checker and script printing features.
- **Autosave**: PowerShell ISE automatically saves any open script file and runspaces; so in case of a crash or failure in your ISE or an unplanned system restart, ISE will restore all your runspaces once you re-open it (it is similar to **Restore last session** in Internet Explorer).
- **The Show-Command cmdlet**: The `Show-Command` cmdlet allows you to display the command in a GUI as if you are browsing a web form or a normal Windows program. You can use `Show-Command` to compose a command in a GUI form; select the required variables and parameters and write the values, and then click on **Run** to execute the command with the parameters supplied in the information field. You can also click on the **Copy** button to copy the command with the parameters and values to the clipboard, so that you can paste it to another PowerShell console and/or save it to a script.

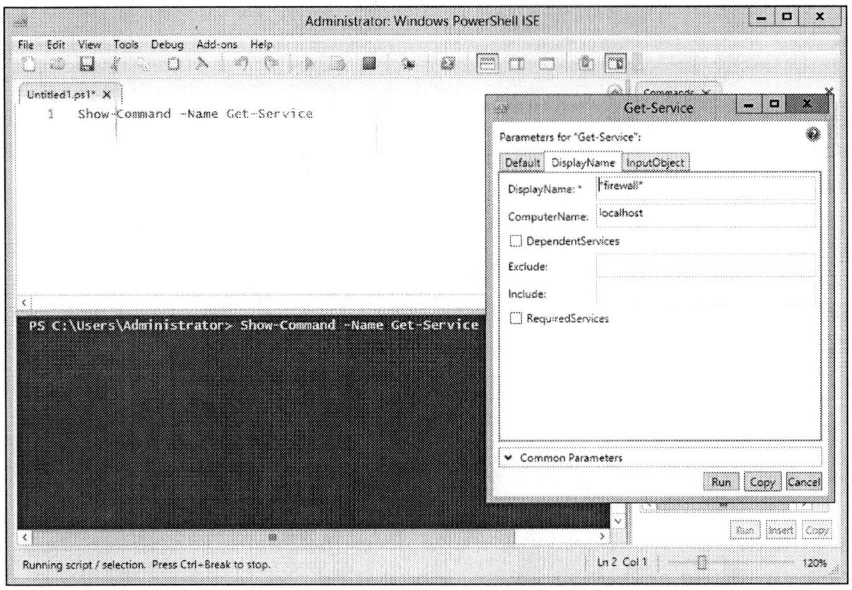

The key features of Windows PowerShell

At the time of writing these lines, Windows PowerShell is available in its fourth release, which comes with a lot of features and enhancements. In this section, we will focus the spotlight on the key features that have a great impact on Windows PowerShell's users in order to understand the essence of PowerShell; then we will make sure to cover these features deeply alongside other features as we go through this book.

- **PowerShell remoting**: The remoting feature allows the execution of PowerShell cmdlets on remote systems that help to manage a set of remote computers from one single machine. The remote execution feature rely on WinRM technology. PowerShell remoting is acting like a Remote Desktop session; you can disconnect your session without interrupting any running process, application, or script and you connect to this session again from the same or a different computer to continue working from where you left off.
- **Background job**: PowerShell introduced the concept of background jobs, which run cmdlets and scripts asynchronously on local and remote machines in the background without affecting the interface or interacting with the console.
- **Scheduled job**: A scheduled job is similar to a background job; both jobs are running asynchronously in the background without interrupting the user interface, but the difference is that a background job must be started manually. However, scheduled jobs can create the background job and schedule it for a later execution using a set of cmdlets instead of doing it manually using the Task Scheduler wizard. You can also get the results of running scheduled jobs and resume the interrupted jobs.
- **Steppable pipeline**: This allows the splitting of script blocks into a separate steppable pipeline. It gives you the option to call the begin, process, and end methods of a script block in order to ease the control of execution sequence.
- **Script debugging**: As in Visual Studio, you can set breakpoints on lines, columns, functions, variables, and commands. You can also specify actions to run when the breakpoint is hit. Stepping into, over, or out of functions is also supported; you can even get the call stack.
- **Error-handling**: PowerShell provides error-handling mechanism through the `Try{ }`, `Catch{ }`, and `Finally { }` statements as in .NET languages.
- **Constrained runspaces**: Constrained runspaces allow creation of PowerShell runspaces with a set of constraints that include the ability to restrict access and execution of cmdlets, scripts, and language elements.

- **Tab-expansion**: This feature is an implementation of autocompletion that completes the cmdlets, properties, and parameter names once the *Tab* button has been pressed.
- **Windows PowerShell Web Access**: A web-based version of the PowerShell console has been introduced in Windows Server 2012, where you can run and execute PowerShell cmdlets from any web browser that is not only available on desktops but also on any mobile or tablet devices.
- **Windows PowerShell Web Service (PSWS)**: This is also known as Management OData IIS Extension, is the infrastructure for creating RESTful ASP.NET web service endpoints that expose management data accessed through PowerShell cmdlets and scripts. These endpoints can be accessed via OData protocol, which allows IT professionals and developers to access the management data remotely from both Windows and non-Windows devices. It simply processes the OData requests and converts them to PowerShell cmdlets invocations.
- **Online and Updateable help**: PowerShell help is no longer shipped in the box. **Help** now can be retrieved and updated from time to time to make sure that you always have the latest help documentation instead of static content that might have some mistakes and errors.
- **Windows PowerShell Workflow**: Workflow capabilities have been introduced in Windows PowerShell 3.0, and it is designed specifically to help you perform long-time and effort-consuming complex tasks across multiple and different devices at different locations.
- **Desired State Configuration** (**DSC**): The DSC feature enables the deployment and management of configuration for software and services to ensure the consistency of configuration data across all computers and devices.

PowerShell fundamentals – back to basics

Now, after understating what is Windows PowerShell and what makes it a unique and different shell, it is time to go back to important basic aspects such as syntax and grammar. Since you are already a .NET developer, and Windows PowerShell syntax is adapted from C#, this part should not take much time.

Working with objects

As mentioned earlier, one of the biggest advantages of PowerShell is being an object-based shell. Everything in PowerShell is an object (.NET object) that is an instance of a .NET framework class. Each object holds a piece of data alongside information about the object itself, in addition to the group of properties and methods. This makes the object manipulation much faster and easier unlike the other traditional text-based shells. Text-based shells produce everything as raw text that requires a lot of parsing and manual manipulation to find the required value at the right location. This is more than enough to turn your tasks into nightmares.

Windows PowerShell is taking advantage of the underlying .NET framework to deal with and manipulate different types of objects such as WMI, COM, XML, and ADSI.

The following examples demonstrate how Windows PowerShell cmdlets are tightly close to the .NET framework. In the following example, we will use the `Get-Date` cmdlet to retrieve the current system time. Yes, you are right. It is what you are thinking of.

```
PS C:\> Get-Date
Wednesday, October 9, 2013 7:57:18 PM
```

Now, we have the result of execution and this is supposed to be a `DateTime` type of object. So, to get the data type of our results, we will use the `GetType()` method.

```
PS C:\> (Get-Date).GetType()

IsPublic IsSerial Name                                     BaseType
-------- -------- ----                                     --------
True     True     DateTime                                 System.ValueType
```

Since we have a .NET object of type `DateTime`, we can use a method such as `ToShortDateString()` to manipulate the result's format.

```
PS C:\> (Get-Date).ToShortDateString()
10/9/2013

PS C:\> (Get-Date).ToShortDateString().GetType()

IsPublic IsSerial Name                                     BaseType
-------- -------- ----                                     --------
True     True     String                                   System.Object
```

Understanding the piping and pipelines

Pipelines are the mechanism used to connect a group of simple cmdlets together in order to build a complex task-based script. A pipeline is not something invented newly for PowerShell, it is an old trick used in different shells before. However, what makes it different here is using objects to make the output of each cmdlet to be used as an input for the next cmdlet in the pipeline. Thus, there is no need of manual result manipulations. For piping, we use the pipeline operator | between cmdlets.

```
PS> cmdlet1 | cmdlet2 -parameter1 argument1 | cmdlet3 -parameter1
  argument1 argument2
```

The following examples demonstrate how to pipe the `Get-Process` cmdlet in different scenarios with other cmdlets using pipelines.

In the first example, the `Get-Process` cmdlet is to be used with the `Get-Member` cmdlet to discover the .NET object class and members type.

```
PS C:\> Get-Process | Get-Member

   TypeName: System.Diagnostics.Process

Name                    MemberType     Definition
----                    ----------     ----------
Handles                 AliasProperty  Handles = Handlecount
Name                    AliasProperty  Name = ProcessName
VM                      AliasProperty  VM = VirtualMemorySize
Close                   Method         void Close()
Kill                    Method         void Kill()
Start                   Method         bool Start()
ProcessName             Property       string ProcessName {get;}
(...)
```

Another piping example: the `Get-Process` cmdlet is to be used with the `Sort-Object` cmdlet to retrieve the list of running processes and sort them according to the CPU usage, and then pipe the results to the `Select-Object` cmdlet to select the top three processes. Finally, the results are formatted using the `Format-Table` cmdlet.

```
PS C:\> Get-Process | Sort-Object -Property CPU -Descending |
  Select-Object -First 4 -Property
  ProcessName,CPU,VirtualMemorySize | Format-Table

ProcessName             CPU                     VirtualMemorySize
-----------             ---                     -----------------
WINWORD                 2155.515625             632963072
OUTLOOK                 1431.640625             792113152
explorer                591.4375                1018482688
```

Understanding and using aliases

Aliases are mainly used as pointers for cmdlets in order to make it easy to remember long commands or to make your commands look familiar. At the end, aliases are used to make your scripting environment more comfortable, friendly, and familiar.

For example, the `Get-ChildItem` cmdlet is the directory listing cmdlet in PowerShell and you will find this cmdlet has two aliases: one called `dir` for people with cmd background and another alias called `ls` for people with UNIX background.

Other examples are `Select-Object`, `Where-Object`, and `Sort-Object` cmdlets that have aliases without the `-Object` part.

So, consider the following command:

```
Get-Process | Sort-Object -Property CPU -Descending | Select-Object
-First 5 -Property ProcessName,CPU,VirtualMemorySize | Format-Table
```

The previous command should be like this after using aliases:

```
gps | Sort -Property CPU -Des | Select -First 5 -Property ProcessName,
CPU,VirtualMemorySize | FT
```

In order to list all available aliases on your system, you have to use the `Get-Alias` cmdlet.

```
PS C:\> Get-Alias

CommandType     Name
-----------     ----
Alias           % -> ForEach-Object
Alias           ? -> Where-Object
Alias           cat -> Get-Content
Alias           cd -> Set-Location
Alias           clc -> Clear-Content
Alias           clear -> Clear-Host
Alias           clhy -> Clear-History
Alias           clv -> Clear-Variable
(...)
```

Also, you can create your own alias using the `New-Alias` and `Set-Alias` cmdlets.

```
PS C:\> New-Alias -Name Restart -Value Restart-Computer

PS C:\> Get-Alias restart

CommandType     Name
-----------     ----
Alias           Restart -> Restart-Computer
```

> Aliases in PowerShell are not persistent, which means that you will lose them once you close your PowerShell session. To avoid this trap, use the `Export-Alias` cmdlet to export all your aliases before closing your session, and then use the `Import-Alias` cmdlet to import them again. To avoid importing your aliases each and every time you open PowerShell console, it is highly preferred to use PowerShell Profiles.

Using variables and data types

In Windows PowerShell, variables are defined as in PHP using the dollar sign (`$`) as a prefix for the variable's name that can contain characters, numeric values, or both, such as `$var`, `$arr4`, and so on.

> *"We wanted to close the semantic gap between what admins thought and what they had to type."*

Jeffrey Snover – PowerShell inventor

Windows PowerShell is a dynamic language. Thus, using data types is optional not because it is a typeless language but because it is a type-promiscuous language. This means that Windows PowerShell interpreter is capable of and smart enough to determine the type of each object and convert them to match each other without any loss of data or object characteristics in order to provide you with the results you expect.

To show you by example, let's define a couple of variables and assign a value with a different data type to each one of them, and then perform a simple mathematical operation on those variables.

```
PS C:\> $a = 1 ; $a.GetType()

IsPublic IsSerial Name                                     BaseType
-------- -------- ----                                     --------
True     True     Int32                                    System.ValueType

PS C:\> $b = "2" ; $b.GetType()

IsPublic IsSerial Name                                     BaseType
-------- -------- ----                                     --------
True     True     String                                   System.Object

PS C:\> $c = 3.5 ; $c.GetType()

IsPublic IsSerial Name                                     BaseType
-------- -------- ----                                     --------
True     True     Double                                   System.ValueType

PS C:\> $a + $b + $c
6.5
```

> Semicolon in PowerShell is optional; however, you might use them to execute multiple commands separately in a single line.

So, we had different variables of the `Int32`, `String`, and `Double` data types, and we were able to calculate them together in just a single step without any data type conversion or casting.

If you feel that using variables this way is confusing, then I have to tell you that you are still able to use strong type variables. All you have to do is just use the data type you need within square brackets like this [data type].

Windows PowerShell is shipped with a set of predefined built-in variables. Those variables can be categorized into the following two categories:

- **Session configuration**: These variables are used to store the current Windows PowerShell session configuration, such as errors generated during a session and user-defined variables
- **Preferences settings**: These variables are used to store the PowerShell preferences and settings such as User Home Folder location, PowerShell Host configuration, and PowerShell version information

You can access those built-in variables either by using the variable name directly, such as `$PSVersionTable`, or using the `$Variable:` prefix with a variable name such as `$Variable:Host` or `$Variable:Error`. You can also list all the variables using the `Get-Variable` cmdlet.

Comparison and logical operators

Windows PowerShell provides different types of operator. You will find part of it very familiar and has been used in different programming languages, and the other part very unique to PowerShell.

The following are examples of the available operators in PowerShell:

- **Arithmetic operators**: The arithmetic operators are add (`+`), subtract (`-`), multiply (`*`), divide (`/`), and mod (`%`)
- **Comparison operators**: The comparison operators are equal (`-eq`), not equal (`-ne`), less than (`-lt`), greater than (`-gt`), less than or equal (`-le`), greater than or equal (`-ge`), contain (`-contains`), and not contain (`-notcontains`)

- **Wildcard and RegEx match operators**: These operators are `-like`, `-notlike`, `-match`, `-notmatch`, and `-replace`
- **Logical and bitwise operators**: These operators are `-and`, `-or`, `-xor`, `-not`, `-band`, `-bor`, `-bxor`, and `-bnot`

Working with arrays and hash tables

Arrays in PowerShell are simply a zero-based list of objects. Also, they are variables of `[Array]` data type as in .NET but as usual PowerShell is developed to code less and get more output; thus there is no need to define the data type even for arrays. The array can be defined using the `@()` syntax or you simply create a variable and assign the list to it, and PowerShell will understand and determine the data type automatically as discussed before.

```
PS C:\> $arr = @()

PS C:\> $arr = 1,2,3,4,5

PS C:\> $arr.GetType()

IsPublic IsSerial Name                                     BaseType
-------- -------- ----                                     --------
True     True     Object[]                                 System.Array
```

Also, arrays can store either single or mixed types of data, as shown in the following example:

```
PS C:\> $arr = 1,'a', ,(Get-Service)

PS C:\> $arr
1
a

Status   Name               DisplayName
------   ----               -----------
Running  AppIDSvc           Application Identity
Running  Appinfo            Application Information
```

Hash tables are similar to arrays in the way they behave and also how we create them. Hash tables are defined using `@{}`, or like arrays just create a variable and fill it with data.

```
PS C:\> $ht = @{}

PS C:\> $ht.GetType()
```

```
IsPublic IsSerial Name                                     BaseType
-------- -------- ----                                     --------
True     True     Hashtable                                System.Object

PS C:\> $ht = @{1='red';2='blue';3='green'} ; $ht

Name                           Value
----                           -----
3                              green
2                              blue
1                              red

PS C:\> $ht.2
blue
```

Script flow and execution control

Flow control and conditional execution in Windows PowerShell is very similar to the C-languages family.

Conditional execution

For conditional execution, PowerShell is using the `if-else` statements and switch cases.

- The `If-else` statement:

```
If (condition)
{
  Statement block
}
ElseIf (condition)
{
  Statement block
}
Else
{
  Statement block
}
```

- The `Switch` case:

```
Switch (pattern)
{
  Pattern {statement block}
```

```
    Pattern {statement block}
    Default {statement block}
  }
```

The preceding code block shows the traditional syntax for the switch case as is used in different programming languages as well as PowerShell. The unique feature in PowerShell is that you can add an extra matching option (condition) to your pattern. The available options are `-regex`, `-wildcard`, `-exact`, and `-casesensitive`.

```
Switch -option (pattern)
{
  Pattern {statement block}
  Pattern {statement block}
  Default {statement block}
}
```

Iterations statements

Iterations (looping) statements in PowerShell work similar to C#.

- The `For` loop:

  ```
  For (initialization; condition; increment)
  {
    Statement block
  }
  ```

- The `ForEach` loop:

  ```
  ForEach (variable in expression)
  {
    Statement block
  }
  ```

- The `While` loop:

  ```
  While (condition)
  {
    Statement block
  }
  ```

- The `Do/While` loop:

  ```
  Do
  {
    Statement block
  }
  While (condition)
  ```

Using functions

Functions remain the same across different programming and scripting languages. They do the same job, which is producing a piece of code with a name that is independent from the main program and can be called any time on demand. This helps in avoiding the routine of repeating the same piece of code more than once in the same program. The keyword `function` is used to define functions in PowerShell.

So, the function syntax should look like the following code:

```
Function <function_name> (function_parameters)
{
  <function_body>
}
```

Let's turn this dummy function syntax into something more practical. No, not a `Hello World..!` function. I meant something that sounds interesting and takes inputs and returns a value. Let's build a quick function called `Avg` that calculates the average of three integer numbers, `n1`, `n2`, and `n3`.

```
Function Avg ([int] $n1, [int] $n2, [int] $n3)
{
  return ($n1 + $n2 + $n3) / 3
}
```

> Using `return` in the previous example is optional; you can remove it and you will get the same result. For more information, return to see the conceptual help *about_Return* topic.

Now, in order to call your function, just use the function name and pass the required values to the respective parameters. The parameters must be passed within the command delimited by a space, unlike other languages in which parameters are delimited by semicolons.

```
PS C:\> Avg -n1 5 -n2 6 -n3 7
6
```

> You can also call your function directly by specifying the parameters' names by position, as shown in the following line of code:
>
> ```
> PS C:\> Avg 5 6 7
> ```

> PowerShell will understand that you are passing values to the parameters and thus will take care to pass each value to each parameter in sequence.

Understanding providers and drives

Providers in Windows PowerShell are .NET libraries that you can use to navigate to data that a particular provider represents. Simply, it is an interface between the user and the data. For instance, `FileSystem` is the provider of all files and folders on your hard disk drive. While `Registry` is also a provider, but for all the registry keys.

Let's have a closer look at the providers by listing all the available providers using the `Get-PSProvider` cmdlet.

```
PS C:\> Get-PSProvider

Name                 Capabilities                      Drives
----                 ------------                      ------
Alias                ShouldProcess                     {Alias}
Environment          ShouldProcess                     {Env}
FileSystem           Filter, Credentials               {C, D, E}
Function             ShouldProcess                     {Function}
Registry             ShouldProcess, Transactions       {HKLM, HKCU}
Variable             ShouldProcess                     {Variable}
Certificate          ShouldProcess                     {Cert}
WSMan                Credentials                       {WSMan}
```

In the previous example, you will notice that each provider has at least one drive. PowerShell providers allow access to their data in the form of drives, so you use the same cmdlets to navigate different objects according to the provider. For example, the `Get-ChildItem` cmdlet will list all the files and folders in the `FileSystem` provider, all registry keys in the Registry provider, and so on.

Let's see how we can access those drivers. By default, you are being redirected to the `FileSystem` provider drive once you open your PowerShell console. To move between different drives, use the `Set-Location` cmdlet.

For example, to navigate to the certificates drive, use the `Set-Location` cmdlet with a drive name `Cert:\` and then use the `Get-ChildItem` cmdlet to list the available certificate stores, or you can simply use it directly as `Get-ChildItem Cert:\`.

```
PS C:\> Set-Location cert:\
PS Cert:\> Get-ChildItem

Location   : CurrentUser
StoreNames : {TrustedPublisher, ClientAuthIssuer, Root, UserDS...}

Location   : LocalMachine
StoreNames : {TrustedPublisher, ClientAuthIssuer, Remote Desktop,
  Root...}
```

Use the `Get-PSDrive` cmdlet to list all the available providers' drives.

Working with script files

The typical PowerShell script file is just a text file with the `.ps1` extension that contains pieces of Windows PowerShell code and instructions. This file could be created using any text editor, even Notepad. However, to make our life easier, we use one of the PowerShell consoles or at least a PowerShell-oriented text editor such as Notepad++.

You can consider the `.ps1` script file in the scripting world as equivalent to your `.exe` file for your .NET application. The PowerShell script files are similar to functions; both can allow users to pass parameters for initialization. Script files have the built-in `$args` variable set up with the parameters passed at the time of the execution.

The following is an example code for using `$args` to get the arguments' values:

```
$firstName = $args[0]
$lastName = $args[1]
Write-Host "Hello, $firstName $lastName"
```

Copy and paste the previous code into your PowerShell editor and save it in a script file called `Greeting.ps1`.

Now, very soon we will have a simple script file that can be executed. The first thing to do right before executing your first script is defining your PowerShell execution policy. Execution policy is a security policy that defines how PowerShell scripts should be executed on your system. The execution policy configuration could be one of the following:

- **Restricted**: In this, no script execution is allowed. This is the default execution policy for Windows Server 2012, Windows 8, and earlier Windows versions.
- **RemoteSigned**: In this, script execution is allowed only for the scripts you wrote on the local computer but not for any scripts from the external sources such as the Internet. The external scripts will not be executed unless they are signed by a trusted publisher. This is the default policy on Windows Server 2012 R2 and Windows 8.1.
- **AllSigned**: In this, all the scripts must be signed by a trusted publisher, even the scripts you wrote on the local computer.
- **Unrestriced**: In this, all scripts can be executed without any restriction.

To set the execution policy settings, we use the `Set-ExecutionPolicy` cmdlet in a Windows PowerShell session running with administrative privileges.

```
PS C:\ > Set-ExecutionPolicy -ExecutionPolicy RemoteSigned
```

Now, your PowerShell console is ready to execute your script file. If you tried to run the script by clicking on it, your script will be opened in Notepad. Don't worry, you did not do anything wrong, but this behavior is one of the security features of Windows PowerShell that prevents you from accidentally running PowerShell scripts. This way it prevents the accidental execution of a script that might harm your computer. Instead, we call the script file from the PowerShell console itself.

In order to call your script, either type the full path of your script or use the `.\` prefix before the script name to refer to the full path if your script is located in the directory you are currently browsing. I know this looks weird but, again, this is for your security to make sure that you are executing the right script and not another script with the same name created by someone or even a malicious code.

```
PS C:\> D:\myScripts\Greetings.ps1 Sherif Talaat
Hello, Sherif Talaat

PS D:\myScripts> .\Greetings.ps1 Sherif Talaat
Hello, Sherif Talaat
```

Comments in PowerShell

Like any programming or scripting language, you can add comments in your code. There are two types of comments in PowerShell:

- **Single-line**: This is used for single (one) line comments. It is represented by the `#` symbol in the beginning of the line.
- **Multi-line block**: This is used for multiple line comments. The comment block starts with the `<#` tag and ends with the `#>` tag.

Using help in Windows PowerShell

PowerShell comes with a super powerful and unique help mechanism. It provides information beyond the traditional help system that shows only the command and its parameters. Help in PowerShell is enough to know everything about what you are looking for; it gives you a synopsis, detailed description, syntax, parameters, input and output objects, notes, examples, and more.

In order to use this help system, we use the `Get-Help` cmdlet along with the respective cmdlet you want to get help for. For example, if you want to show help information for the `Get-Process` cmdlet, the code should looks like the following:

```
PS C:\> Get-Help Get-Process
```

The previous line of code will show basic help information about the `Get-Process` cmdlet. You can add extra parameters to get more information. For instance, you can add `-detailed` or `-Full` to get a detailed help information.

```
PS C:\> Get-Help Get-Process -Detailed
```

If you know the cmdlet but want just a few examples to help you to get started with the syntax, then you can add `-Examples` to show the examples only.

```
PS C:\> Get-Help Get-Process -Examples
```

Last but not least, reading long pieces of information on the console window is hard. The more information you get, the harder you read. For this purpose, PowerShell has the `-ShowWindow` parameter that displays the help information on a GUI instead of the console, as shown in the following screenshot:

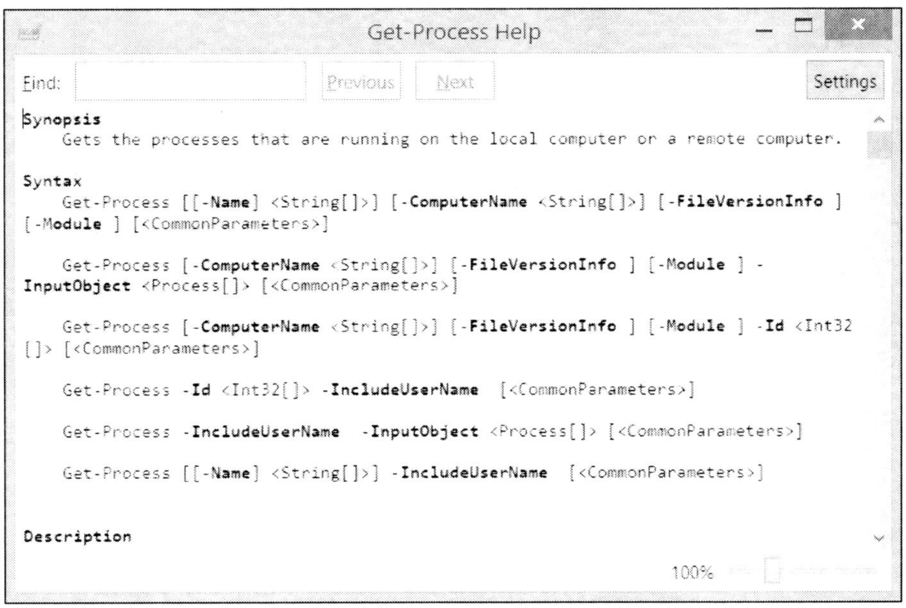

Another interesting feature in PowerShell help is the conceptual **About** help topics. These topics are extra help information about PowerShell modules and other PowerShell subjects such as syntax. They are called About topics because it always starts with `about_` as a prefix.

The following code demonstrates how to get the list of all the available help files in your system:

```
PS C:\> Get-Help -Category HelpFile

Name                              Category
----                              --------
about_ActivityCommonParameters    HelpFile
about_Aliases                     HelpFile
about_Arithmetic_Operators        HelpFile
about_Arrays                      HelpFile
(...)
```

The information in the help topics can be retrieved by using the `Get-Help` cmdlet along with the topic name.

```
PS C:\> Get-Help about_Functions
```

Earlier in this chapter, we mentioned that starting with Version 3, PowerShell help is no longer a shipped inbox. However, it is downloaded and updated from the Internet. For the purposes of achieving this task, we use a couple of cmdlets such as `Update-Help` and `Save-Help`. The `Update-Help` cmdlet is used to download the latest help files directly from the Internet and embed them in PowerShell. However, the `Save-Help` cmdlet downloads the help files and stores them on a local disk or shared folder. So, you can use them later to update the help files locally instead of downloading them from the Internet each time for every computer.

```
PS C:\> Save-Help -DestinationPath \\FS01.contoso.local\ PSHelp
PS C:\> Update-Help -SourcePath \\FS01.contoso.local\PSHelp
```

Downloading the example code

You can download the example code files for all Packt books you have purchased from your account at `http://www.packtpub.com`. If you purchased this book elsewhere, you can visit `http://www.packtpub.com/support` and register to have the files e-mailed directly to you.

PowerShell's common parameters

Common parameters are the set of cmdlet parameters that are available for any cmdlet. These parameters are implemented and handled by Windows PowerShell and not by a cmdlet developer. The developer has to populate and pass the data to the parameters within the cmdlet code.

The common parameters in PowerShell are:

- `Verbose`: This displays detailed information about the operation performed by the cmdlet. You can think of it as a tracing or logging parameter.
- `Debug`: This is similar to `verbose` but it displays a programmer-level information about the operation performed by the cmdlet.
- `ErrorAction`: This determines how the cmdlets respond to the non-terminating error from the cmdlet during execution. This parameter has pre-defined values, which are `Continue`, `ignore`, `inquire`, `stop`, `suspend`, and `SilentlyContinue`.
- `ErrorVariable`: This determines a variable to store the error messages generated by the cmdlet during the execution of an operation.
- `WarningAction`: This determines how the cmdlets respond to the warning from the cmdlet during execution. This parameter has fewer pre-defined values such as `ErrorAction`. The values are `Continue`, `stop`, `inquire`, and `SilentlyContinue`.
- `WarningVariable`: This determines a variable to store the warning messages generated by a cmdlet during the operation execution.
- `WhatIf`: This displays a message that describes the instructions, effects, and change in effects that are supposed to happen by the cmdlet without executing it.
- `Confirm`: This prompts for a confirmation before executing cmdlets.
- `OutBuffer`: This determines the number of objects to be accumulated in the buffer before moving to the next cmdlet in the pipeline.
- `OutVariable`: This determines the variable to store the output objects from the cmdlet.

> You can also get more information and examples about the common parameters using `PS :\> Get-Help about_CommonParameters`.

Summary

In this chapter, we learned what Windows PowerShell is, what makes it a different shell, and how it is impacting IT professionals and developers. Also, we got introduced to the Windows PowerShell console and to the ISE. Then we shed the light on the objects structure and on how PowerShell is using the underlying .NET framework to deal with and manipulate objects. Moreover, we had a quick tour of PowerShell syntax and grammar and how it is very close to the C# syntax.

In the next chapter, we will jump into more advanced PowerShell topics, for example, working with different objects such as WMI, CIM, and COM+, understanding scripting debugging, error-handling techniques in PowerShell, and developing PowerShell modules and workflows.

2
Unleashing Your Development Skills with PowerShell

Windows PowerShell is a game changer in the shell scripting and automation world. This is not only because it is an object-based scripting language that is built on top of the .NET framework but also because it unifies a lot of different scripting and automation tools in one single, consistent, and dynamic engine. By leveraging the same engine and language you can deal with various amazing technologies such as **Windows Management Instrumentation** (**WMI**), **Common Information Model** (**CIM**), and **Component Object Model** (**COM**). Moreover, you can use it to build an automation interface for the applications you develop.

In this chapter, we will go deeper into Windows PowerShell to understand what are the different technologies that can be managed by Windows PowerShell, learn how to do it, and discover more advanced scripting techniques obtained from your current development skills.

In this chapter, we will cover the following topics:

- The basics of WMI, CIM, COM, and XML
- Extending Windows PowerShell capabilities with .NET, COM, XML, and WMI
- Understanding Windows PowerShell Modules
- Developing Windows PowerShell Modules
- Script debugging and error handling

Understanding CIM and WMI

CIM is an open standard defined by the **Distributed Management Task Force (DMTF)** as part of the **Web-Based Enterprise Management (WBEM)** initiative. CIM is used to define an extensible data model that describes, processes, and obtains the characteristic information of managed resources such as hardware components and software. CIM is a programming model that is object oriented and manufacture independent, which means that you can manage different resources from different vendors by just using the CIM standard. On the other side, WMI is a Microsoft implementation of CIM that is introduced in Windows 2000 to allow the management of all Windows software and hardware components.

CIM and WMI in Windows PowerShell

Windows PowerShell v2.0 has been shipped with a few cmdlets to support and work with WMI as a middle layer between the end user (system administrators and developers) and CIM. Later on, in Windows PowerShell v3.0, a new direct support to CIM was introduced via more cmdlets with Windows Server 2012 and Windows 8, which allows PowerShell users to directly expose the CIM schema and data model.

To retrieve the list of cmdlets for WMI and CIM, we will use the `Get-Command` cmdlet with the `-Name` parameter filtered by a wildcard and the `-Type` parameter, filtered by a cmdlet argument to get only the cmdlets and not functions or aliases, as shown in the following snippet:

```
#List all WMI available Cmdlets
PS C:\> Get-Command *WMI* -Type Cmdlet

CommandType     Name                 ModuleName
-----------     ----                 ----------
Cmdlet          Get-WmiObject        Microsoft.PowerShell.Management
Cmdlet          Invoke-WmiMethod     Microsoft.PowerShell.Management
Cmdlet          Register-WmiEvent    Microsoft.PowerShell.Management
Cmdlet          Remove-WmiObject     Microsoft.PowerShell.Management
Cmdlet          Set-WmiInstance      Microsoft.PowerShell.Management
#List all CIM available Cmdlets
PS C:\> Get-Command *CIM* -Type Cmdlet

CommandType     Name                        ModuleName
-----------     ----                        ----------
Cmdlet          Get-CimAssociatedInstance        CimCmdlets
Cmdlet          Get-CimClass                     CimCmdlets
Cmdlet          Get-CimInstance                  CimCmdlets
```

```
Cmdlet          Get-CimSession                   CimCmdlets
Cmdlet          Invoke-CimMethod                 CimCmdlets
Cmdlet          New-CimInstance                  CimCmdlets
Cmdlet          New-CimSession                   CimCmdlets
Cmdlet          New-CimSessionOption             CimCmdlets
Cmdlet          Register-CimIndicationEvent      CimCmdlets
Cmdlet          Remove-CimInstance               CimCmdlets
Cmdlet          Remove-CimSession                CimCmdlets
Cmdlet          Set-CimInstance                  CimCmdlets
```

Now, after getting the list of both cmdlets for CIM and WMI, take a few seconds for looking at each cmdlet. Did you notice it? Yes, there are CIM cmdlets similar to WMI cmdlets, which makes sense because, as we said earlier, WMI is an implementation of CIM.

Although both the cmdlet sets look the same and show almost the same results, you will find that the CIM-related cmdlets have more parameters and there are even more cmdlets than in WMI in order to provide you with more information.

CIM and WMI represent the provided information in the form of namespaces and classes. For example, there is a class for BIOS called `Win32_BIOS`, and another one for the operating system called `Win32_OperatingSystem`. There are other classes that start with _, such as `_CLASSNAME` for internal operating system usage and `CIM_CLASSNAME` for some basic classes, but the classes that are mostly used are the ones that start with the prefix `Win32_CLASSNAME`.

In case you do not know the name of a class or want to discover the list of available classes in your system, you can use either the `Get-WmiObject -List` cmdlet or the `Get-CimClass` cmdlet to retrieve the same results.

```
#List available classes using WMI
PS C:\> Get-WmiObject -Class * -List

#List available classes using CIM
PS C:\> Get-CimClass -ClassName *
Win32_CurrentTime
Win32_LocalTime
Win32_OperatingSystem
Win32_Process
Win32_ComputerSystem
Win32_BIOS
Win32_SoftwareElement
 (...)

#Comparing the number of classes retrieved by each cmdlet
```

```
PS C:\> (Get-WmiObject -List).count -eq (Get-CimClass).count
True
```

After knowing which class you want to use, you have to create an instance of this class to get whatever information is provided by it. For this purpose, you can use either the `Get-WmiObject` cmdlet or the `Get-CimInstance` cmdlet and define the class name as a parameter.

```
#Get class instance using WMI
PS C:\> Get-WmiObject -Class Win32_BIOS

#Create class instance using CIM
PS C:\> Get-CimInstance -ClassName Win32_BIOS

SMBIOSBIOSVersion : 8BET59WW (1.39 )
Manufacturer      : LENOVO
Name              : Default System BIOS
SerialNumber      : R9T081V
Version           : LENOVO - 1390
```

You can also use `-Query` as a parameter instead of a class name to execute a predefined WMI query written in **WMI Query Language (WQL)**.

```
#Building WQL query to read from Win32_NetworkAdapter class
PS C:\> $Query = "Select * From Win32_NetworkAdapter Where Name like
'%Intel%'"

#Execute the WQL query using WMI
PS C:\> Get-WmiObject -Query $Query | Select DeviceID, Name

#Execute the WQL query using CIM
PS C:\> Get-CimInstance -Query $Query | Select DeviceID, Name

DeviceID                  Name
--------                  ----
0                         Intel(R) 82579LM Gigabit Network Connection
2                         Intel(R) Centrino(R) Ultimate-N 6300 AGN
```

You can follow the same steps as in the previous example when you want to remove an instance. Use the `Remove-WmiObject` and `Remove-CimInstance` cmdlets as well as `Set-WmiInstance` and `Set-CimInstance` when you want to update an existing instance. The following simple example will show how we can use the `Get-WmiObject` and `Remove-WmiObject` cmdlets together to get a specific directory information in a WMI instance, and then delete it:

```
#Get a directory called "myOldBackup'
$folder = Get-WmiObject -Class Win32_Directory -Filter "Name='D:\\
myOldBackup'"
```

```
#Remove (delete) the folder
$folder | Remove-WmiObject
```

Other interesting cmdlets are `Register-CimIndicationEvent` and `Register-WmiEvent`; both these cmdlets allow you to trigger an action within a PowerShell scriptblock according to a predefined WMI or CIM event criteria. For example, you can trigger a notification message when the CPU utilization exceeds 85 percent or when a specific service stopped.

More reasons to adopt CIM

Well, after understanding what is WMI and CIM and exploring a few cmdlets with many similarities from both sides, you have to admit that you are getting confused and wondering why new CIM cmdlets have been introduced and why use them if WMI cmdlets were fine in the previous versions of Windows PowerShell.

To answer this question and avoid any philosophical debates, let's discover what makes CIM an added value and feature to PowerShell using the following points:

- It is an open standard, which means that it is not locked into the Windows operating system only, so that you can use CIM to manage other vendors and manufacturers.
- It uses **WS-Management** (**WS-MAN**) protocol for remote management so that you can use it with any remote server or device implementing this protocol. However, WMI is used to manage only Windows over the DCOM protocol.
- It can be used with **Open Management Infrastructure** (**OMI**) compliant devices.

> Read more about OMI from the following article:
> `http://blogs.technet.com/b/windowsserver/archive/2012/06/28/open-management-infrastructure.aspx`

- It can be used to manage any computer or device with an operating system that has the **CIM Object Manager** (**CIMOM**) compliance implemented irrespective of the vendor. So, you can use CIM to manage Windows as well as non-Windows operating systems.

Working with XML

XML parsing and formatting is one of the most commonly used functionalities in application development. PowerShell provides built-in support for XML in a smart way that allows you to work with XML files easily with minimal lines of code. This is enough to make PowerShell your perfect choice for daily XML tasks and operations.

Loading XML files

There are two ways to load an XML file in PowerShell—either using the `Get-Content` cmdlet or using the `Select-Xml` cmdlet with the `XPath` queries.

Using the Get-Content cmdlet

In order to load and read the content of a file in PowerShell, we use the `Get-Content` cmdlet; this cmdlet is used to load content from text as well as XML files, which are text files written in a structured, descriptive format so that the `Get-Content` cmdlet can be used to load the XML files too.

```
#Load file content using Get-Content
PS C:\> Get-Content C:\Employees.xml
```

The previous lines will load the content of the XML file as normal text. So, in order to make PowerShell understand that this is an XML file, we have to either cast the results of the `Get-Content` cmdlet or store the output in a strongly typed variable of XML data type, as shown in the following examples:

```
#results casting
$employee = [xml](Get-Content D:\Employees.xml)

#Store results in XML variable
[xml] $employees = Get-Content D:\Employees.xml
```

The strongly typed variables, such as `[xml] $employees`, can be assigned only with a `System.Xml.XmlDocument` type of object. Otherwise, they will trigger an error.

The following code shows a sample of the `employee.xml` file's structure:

```
<staff>
<branch location="cairo">
  <employee>
    <Name>Sherif Talaat</Name>
    <Role>IT</Role>
  </employee>
</branch>
</staff>
```

The XML file that is loaded has information about the staff members in different branches with different specialties. Now, we have the content of the file stored in a variable called `$employees` that can be accessed normally like any other object along with XML capabilities, as shown in the following examples:

```
#Access child nodes of XML documents
PS C:\> $employees.staff.ChildNodes

location                           employee
--------                           --------
cairo                              {Sherif Talaat, Raymond Elias}
redmond                            {Bill Gates, Steve Jobs}

#Get attributes information of a node
PS C:\> $employees.staff.branch.Get_Attributes()

#text
-----
cairo
Redmond

#Get attributes value by Attribute name
PS C:\> $employees.staff.branch. location
cairo
Redmond

#Change the value of attribute
PS C:\> $employees.staff.branch[0]. location
= 'Seattle'

#Change and Modify Single node
PS C:\> $employees.staff.branch.employee

Name                    Role
----                    ----
Sherif Talaat           IT
Raymond Elias           Technology Specialist

PS C:\> $emp = $employees.staff.branch.employee[0]

PS C:\> $emp.Role = "PowerShell Guru"

PS C:\> $employees.SelectNodes("//employee[Name='Sherif Talaat']")
```

```
Name                    Role
----                    ----
Sherif Talaat           PowerShell Guru

#add new node
PS C:\> $newemployee = $employees.CreateElement("employee")
PS C:\> $newemployee.set_InnerXML("<Name>Ahmad Mofeed</
Name><Role>Security Consultant</Role>")
PS C:\> $employees.staff.branch[0].AppendChild($newemployee)

PS C:\> $employees.staff.branch[0].employee

Name                    Role
----                    ----
Sherif Talaat           PowerShell Guru
Raymond Elias           Technology Specialist
Ahmad Mofeed            Security Consultant
```

Using the Select-Xml cmdlet

Another way to load and work with XML files is using the `Select-Xml` cmdlet that allows you to directly specify the XML file path along with an `XPath` search query to retrieve the respective node and data, as shown in the following snippet:

```
#Get data from XML file using XPath query
PS C:\> Select-Xml -Path D:\Employees.xml -XPath "staff/branch/
employee"

Node                  Path                   Pattern
----                  ----                   -------
employee              D:\Employees.xml       staff/branch/employee
employee              D:\Employees.xml       staff/branch/employee
employee              D:\Employees.xml       staff/branch/employee
```

In the previous example, the `Select-Xml` cmdlet was used to retrieve XML nodes using the `XPath` search query; the result is an object of nodes with no values. To expand these nodes and enumerate their values, we have to use the `Select-Object` cmdlet with the `-ExpandProperty` parameter.

```
PS C:\> Select-Xml -Path D:\Employees.xml -XPath "staff/branch/
employee" | Select-Object -ExpandProperty Node

Name                          Role
----                          ----
```

```
Sherif Talaat                  IT
Raymond Elias                  Technology Specialist
Bill Gates                     Developer
```

Importing and exporting XML files

PowerShell also provides a couple of XML-related cmdlets—the `Export-CliXml` cmdlet to export the object(s) to an XML file and `Import-CliXml` to import and load the file that was previously exported by PowerShell, as shown in the following snippet:

```
#Export object to XML file
PS C:\> Get-Service | Export-Clixml D:\Services.xml

#Import object from XML file
PS C:\> Import-Clixml D:\Services.xml -First 5

Status   Name               DisplayName
------   ----               -----------
Running  AdobeARMservice    Adobe Acrobat Update Service
Stopped  AeLookupSvc        Application Experience
Stopped  ALG                Application Layer Gateway Service
Running  AppIDSvc           Application Identity
Running  Appinfo            Application Information
```

Moreover, you also have the `ConvertTo-Xml` cmdlet that is similar to the `Export-CliXml` cmdlet, where both the cmdlets create an XML representation of one or more objects. The only difference is that the `Export-CliXml` cmdlet stores the XML code in a file while the `ConvertTo-Xml` cmdlet returns an XML object that can be used as an input to another cmdlet.

Working with COM

As is the case with WMI and XML, PowerShell also supports working with the COM type of objects. In this section, we will understand how COM works in PowerShell using two interesting examples that cover COM with Internet Explorer and Microsoft Excel.

Creating an instance of a COM object

In order to create an instance of a COM object, we use the `New-Object` cmdlet with the `-ComObject` parameter and `ProgID` as an argument, where the `ProgID` is the friendly name of the COM class used during class registration. Thus, the final command should look like this:

```
#create new COM object
PS C:\> $com = New-Object -ComObject <ProgID>
```

Automating Internet Explorer with COM and PowerShell

As mentioned earlier, the `ProgID` parameter is required to create a COM object instance of an application. For Internet Explorer, the `ProgID` parameter is `InternetExplorer.Application`; so, let's create a COM object of Internet Explorer and start playing with it.

The first step is to create an object using the `New-Object` cmdlet and store it in a variable called `$ie` to make it easy to work with that object.

```
#Creating new object of IE COM class
PS C:\> $ie = New-Object -ComObject InternetExplorer.Application
```

Then, let's define the properties of this instance. In the case of Internet Explorer, we need to define the IE window's height and width, visibility, URL, and so on.

```
$ie.navigate("about:blank")
$ie.height = 800
$ie.width = 1200
$ie.visible = $true
```

> For more information about Internet Explorer Object Model, please refer to `http://msdn.microsoft.com/en-us/library/ms970456.aspx`.

The previous code will launch an IE window with a blank web page. Is that everything we can do with IE? Of course not; we can do more interesting things. Let's modify this code to browse the `outlook.com` website, find the e-mail address and password textboxes, fill them with data, and click on the **Sign in** button.

First, prompt the user to enter the e-mail address and password using the `Read-Host` cmdlet.

```
$EmailAddress = Read-Host -Prompt "Enter your Microsoft Account.."
```

For the password, make sure to use the `-AsSecureString` parameter in order to enter the password in the form of asterisks instead of clear text and also save the password encrypted in the variable so that no one can read it.

```
$Password = Read-Host -AsSecureString -Prompt "Enter your Password..."
```

The window should look as follows:

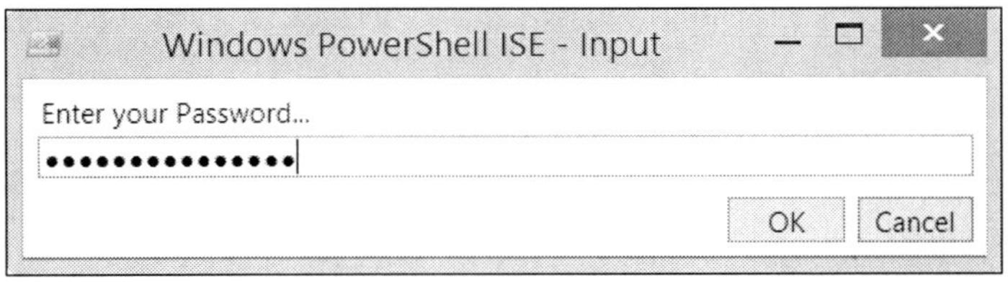

Then, create the COM object and define the properties, but this time make sure to navigate to `outlook.com` instead of a blank web page:

```
$ie = New-Object -ComObject InternetExplorer.Application
$ie.height = 800
$ie.width = 1200
$ie.navigate("http://outlook.com")
$ie.visible = $true
```

To ensure that your script will progress successfully, make sure that your page is successfully loaded before proceeding with the next command.

```
while($ie.Busy){Start-Sleep -Milliseconds 500}
```

Now inspect the web page elements such as textboxes and buttons and fill them with the values received from the user in the beginning. The web page's elements can be inspect using **F12 developer tools** in Internet Explorer.

```
$doc = $ie.document
$tbUsername = $doc.getElementByID("i0116")
$tbUsername.value = $EmailAddress
$tbPassword = $doc.getElementByID("i0118")
$tbPassword.value = $Password
$btnSubmit = $doc.getElementByID("idSIButton9")
```

Finally, trigger the `Click` event on the **Sign in** button.

```
$btnSubmit.Click();
```

Now, you should be looking at your inbox. Isn't it interesting?

Automating Microsoft Excel with COM and PowerShell

Another popular usage of COM is automation of the Microsoft Office suite applications. In this section, we will work with the Microsoft Excel COM class. The same that applies to Excel can also be applied to Word, Access, Outlook, and so on.

In this example, we will build an Excel spreadsheet-based report (as you can see in the following screenshot) that shows the current status of all Windows services that are either running or stopped. The code in the following section describes how can we achieve our target and build our report using the Excel COM interface, `Excel.Application`.

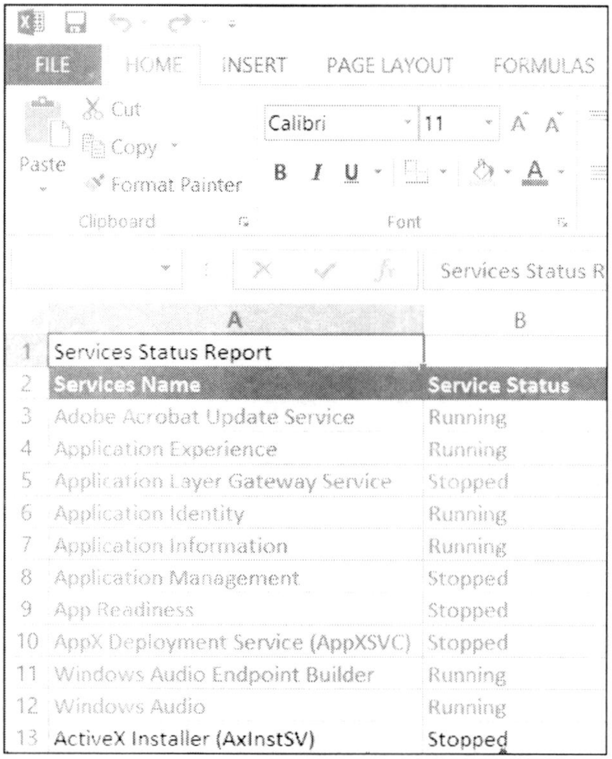

The first step is to create an instance of `Excel.Application`:

```
$Excel = New-Object -ComObject Excel.Application
```

By now, if you have checked the running processes on your Windows, you should have a process for Microsoft Excel, but the Excel window will not launch until you change the visibility of the instance.

```
$Excel.visible = $True
```

Then, we will create a new Excel workbook, and add one worksheet to it.

```
$ExcelWB = $Excel.Workbooks.Add()
$ExcelWS = $ExcelWB.Worksheets.Item(1)
```

Now, we have everything ready, so let's fill the worksheet with data. First, we will create a title for the report in the first two cells in the first row.

```
$ExcelWS.Cells.Item(1,1) = "Services Status Report"
$ExcelWS.Range("A1","B1").Cells.Merge()
```

Then, we will create a header for the table with two columns: **Service Name** and **Service Status** in the second row of the worksheet.

```
$ExcelWS.Cells.Item(2,1) = "Services Name"
$ExcelWS.Cells.Item(2,2) = "Service Status"
```

Then, list all Windows services using the `Get-Service` cmdlet and iterate over this list using the `ForEach` loop to create a new row for each service in the list.

```
$row = 3
ForEach($Service in Get-Service)
{
    $ExcelWS.Cells.Item($row,1) = $Service.DisplayName
    $ExcelWS.Cells.Item($row,2) = $Service.Status.ToString()
    if($Service.Status -eq "Running")
        {
            $ExcelWS.Cells.Item($row,1).Font.ColorIndex = 10
            $ExcelWS.Cells.Item($row,2).Font.ColorIndex = 10
        }
    Elseif($Service.Status -eq "Stopped")
        {
            $ExcelWS.Cells.Item($row,1).Font.ColorIndex = 3
            $ExcelWS.Cells.Item($row,2).Font.ColorIndex = 3
        }
  $row++
}
```

Finally, save the report and quit the Excel instance.

```
$ExcelWS.SaveAs("D:\ServicesStatusReport.xlsx")
$Excel.Quit()
```

For more information about Excel COM interface, refer to http://msdn.microsoft.com/en-us/library/microsoft.office.interop.excel.application.aspx.

Working with .NET objects

In *Chapter 1, Getting Started with Windows PowerShell*, we discussed the relation between Windows PowerShell and the .NET framework, and we saw how .NET is adapted in PowerShell in different examples. In this section of this chapter, we will be working intensely with .NET objects in PowerShell.

Creating .NET objects

In order to create a new .NET object, we usually use the `New-Object` cmdlet that it is similar to the `new` operator in languages such as C#. Yes, I said *usually* because you might use casting to convert a PowerShell object to a .NET object as seen in *Chapter 1, Getting Started with Windows PowerShell*. The `New-Object` cmdlet is used to create .NET objects and COM objects, but the parameters are different in the case of COM objects.

```
PS C:\> $date = New-Object -TypeName System.DateTime -ArgumentList
2013,10,24
PS C:\> $date
Thursday, October 24, 2013 12:00:00 AM
```

You can define the object type directly without using `-TypeName` because it is a positional parameter, thus you can omit it.

```
PS C:\> $string = New-Object System.String -ArgumentList "PowerShell
Rocks!"
PS C:\> $string
PowerShell Rocks!
```

In the previous example, we used the `New-Object` cmdlet to create two new .NET objects of the `DateTime` and `String` datatypes along with the `-ArgumentList` parameter used to pass constructor values.

The code in the previous example is equivalent to the following code:

```
PS C:\> [datetime] $date = "2013/10/24"

PS C:\> [string] $string = " PowerShell Rocks!"
```

Extending .NET objects

You can extend an instance of a .NET object by adding custom properties and members to it using the `Add-Member` cmdlet.

The following example will show how you can use `Add-Member` to add a `NoteProperty` member to an existing object. In this example, we will load an XML file in the `xml` object, and then add a custom member of the type `NoteProperty` called `Description` to store a description about the XML file content.

```
#Load XML file
PS C:\> [xml] $xml = Get-Content D:\Employees.xml

#Add new NoteProperty Member using Add-Member
PS C:\>Add-Member -InputObject $xml -MemberType NoteProperty -Name
Description -Value "Employees information database"

#Show the new added member
PS C:\> $xml | Get-Member -MemberType NoteProperty | fl
TypeName   : System.Xml.XmlDocument
Name       : Description
MemberType : NoteProperty
Definition : System.String Description=Employees information database
```

Another example will show how to add a custom method of the type `ScriptMethod` that will execute a scriptblock against an `array` object. In this example, we will add a custom member called `Censored()` that will check the text and replace any inappropriate word with asterisks:

```
#Creating an array of websites URLs
PS C:\> $websites = @("facebook.com","twitter.com","google.com","xxx.
com")

#Add new ScriptMethod member to the array object
PS C:\> Add-Member -InputObject $websites -MemberType ScriptMethod
-Name Censored -Value {$this -replace "xxx","***"}

#Execute the new added method
PS C:\> $websites.Censored()
facebook.com
twitter.com
google.com
***.com
```

> For more information about the other member types read the articles at `http://msdn.microsoft.com/en-us/library/windows/desktop/system.management.automation.psmembertypes(v=vs.85).aspx`.

Extending .NET framework types

Windows PowerShell allows you to define .NET framework types (classes) so that you can create objects of those classes later on using the `New-Object` cmdlet. These types can be defined by source code file, assembly file, or even an inline code of C#, VB, and JScript.

Defining the object type using an inline C# class

The following example will show how to create a new object type from an inline C# class. First off, we will create a class definition for a basic calculator with four methods representing four arithmetic operations. Then, we will use the `Add-Type` cmdlet to add the new class to the current PowerShell session. Finally, we will create a new object of this class using the `New-Object` cmdlet.

```
PS C:\> $myCalc = @"
public class PSCalc
{
    public int Add(int x, int y) {return x + y;}
    public int Subtract(int x, int y) {return x - y;}
    public int Multiply(int x, int y) {return x * y;}
    public int Divid(int x, int y) {return x / y;}
}
"@

PS C:\> Add-Type -TypeDefinition $myCalc

PS C:\> $op = New-Object PSCalc
```

Now, you can use this `$op` object to execute one of the methods of the defined class.

```
PS C:\> $op.Multiply(4,8)
32
```

Another exciting thing is that you can execute a static method of a class directly in PowerShell. For instance, the `System.Math` class has many static methods; one of them called `Pow()` calculates the power value. To call this method from PowerShell, you should write the following:

```
PS C:\> [System.Math]::Pow(2,4)
```

Defining an object type using an assembly name or file

Another way to define a new object type is using the assembly name (namespace) or the assembly file (DLL), and then using the `New-Object` cmdlet to create the object.

The following example will show how we can add a new type using the assembly namespace:

```
PS C:\> $form = New-Object System.Windows.Forms

New-Object : Cannot find type [System.Windows.Forms]: verify that the
assembly containing this type is loaded.
At line:1 char:8
+ $form = New-Object System.Windows.Forms
+         ~~~~~~~~~~~~~~~~~~~~~~~~~~~~~~~~~
    + CategoryInfo          : InvalidType: (:) [New-Object],
PSArgumentException
    + FullyQualifiedErrorId : TypeNotFound,Microsoft.PowerShell.
Commands.NewObjectCommand
```

In the previous example, we tried to create a strongly typed generic collection using the `New-Object` cmdlet, but we got an error because PowerShell cannot find the assembly that contains this type. So, in order to get over this problem, we have to load the required assembly.

```
PS C:\> Add-Type -AssemblyName System.Windows.Forms
```

Moreover, you can also use the `-Path` parameter instead of `-AssemblyName` to load the classes from the DLL itself.

```
PS C:\> Add-Type -Path D:\myApp\program.dll
```

Understanding Windows PowerShell Modules

Windows PowerShell Modules are the way of organizing and packaging PowerShell scripts and code files into distributable and reusable units. Windows PowerShell comes with a pretty good number of built-in modules that provide cmdlets for almost all Windows Server roles and features. For example, there is a module for Server Manager, Hyper-V, Active Directory, and IIS.

In order to list all the available modules installed on the operating system, we use the `Get-Module` cmdlet with the `-ListAvailable` parameters:

```
PS C:\> Get-Module -ListAvailable | Select Name,Version,ModuleType

Name                    Version            ModuleType
----                    -------            ----------
AppLocker               2.0.0.0            Manifest
AssignedAccess          1.0.0.0            Script
BitLocker               1.0.0.0            Manifest
```

```
Dism                       2.0               Script
DnsClient                  1.0.0.0           Manifest
Hyper-V                    1.1               Binary
(. . .)
```

The previous example shows that there are different types of PowerShell modules; we will cover these types in the next section when we start building new modules.

To start using any module—either a built-in or third-party module—you have to use the Import-Module <Module_Name> cmdlet to import this module first to your current PowerShell session.

```
#Import Hyper-V and AppLocker modules
PS C:\> Import-Module -Name Hyper-V,AppLocker
```

If you are importing a module stored under the default PowerShell modules directory, you can use the module name only as an argument; however, if you are importing a module in a different directory, you have to define the full path of the module. Also, if you are using PowerShell ISE 3.0 or later, and you type a cmdlet name that resides inside a module, this will automatically load that module for you.

> To get the default module's paths, use the environment variable `$env:PSModulePath`.
>
> You can add additional module path `$env:PSModulePath += "; C:\MyModules"`
>
> Read more about `PSModulePath` at `http://msdn.microsoft.com/en-us/library/dd878326(v=vs.85).aspx`

Creating Windows PowerShell Modules

In this section, we will learn by examples the different types of PowerShell modules and how we can create each type.

The script modules

A script module is simply a PowerShell file with (`.psm1`), a file extension that contains a PowerShell code such as functions, variables, and aliases.

To create a script module, we will create a couple of simple functions along with an alias for each one; those functions will do addition and subtraction operations for two numbers, and then will save this script in a file with the extension `.psm1`. The filename will be the module name when you import it.

```
Function Add-Numbers($x,$y)
{
```

```
    $x + $y
}

Function Subtract-Numbers($x,$y)
{
    $x - $y
}

New-Alias -Name an -Value Add-Numbers
New-Alias -Name sn -Value Subtract-Numbers

#Export modules member
Export-ModuleMember -Function * -Alias *
```

In the previous example you will notice that we have used the `Export-ModuleMember` cmdlet at the end of the file. This cmdlet is used to identify PowerShell types such as functions, aliases, and variables to be exported as members of this module while importing this module using the `Import-Module` cmdlet.

```
PS C:\> Import-Module D:\myModules\ScriptModule.psm1 -Force
```

When you import this module, you will receive the following warning:

WARNING: The names of some imported commands from the module 'ScriptModule' include unapproved verbs that might make them less discoverable. To find the commands with unapproved verbs, run the Import-Module command again with the Verbose parameter. For a list of approved verbs, type Get-Verb.

The reason for this warning is that we are using a non-standard (unapproved) verb for our function names. This will not affect the function execution but it is recommended to follow the approved verbs for standardization.

You can get the list of approved verbs and their categories using the `Get-Verb` cmdlet. Also, you can suppress this warning by adding the `-DisableNameChecking` switch.

Now, after loading our module, we will discover it using the `Get-Module` cmdlet.

```
PS C:\> Get-Module ScriptModule | fl

Name              : scriptmodule
Path              : D:\scriptmodule.psm1
ModuleType        : Script
Version           : 0.0
NestedModules     : {}
ExportedFunctions : {Add-Numbers, Subtract-Numbers}
ExportedCmdlets   :
```

```
ExportedVariables :
ExportedAliases   : {an, sn}
```

The binary modules

A binary module is an assembly file (`.DLL`) that contains a compiled code such as cmdlet classes and providers. A very good example of binary modules is the built-in modules in PowerShell.

```
PS C:\> Get-Module -Name Microsoft.PowerShell.* | Select
Name,NestedModules
```

Creating your first binary module

In this section, we will walk you through building a binary module. Unlike other modules, we create and develop the binary modules using Microsoft Visual Studio. In this tutorial, we will create a binary module `MyBinaryModule` that has two cmdlets—the `Get-EvenOrOdd` cmdlet that takes an array of integer values and checks the even and odd numbers, and the `Validate-EmailAddress` cmdlet that takes a string and checks whether it is in a valid e-mail address format or not.

The first step in building our first binary module is creating a class library project in Visual Studio. The current class library name will be the module name later, so let's name our class library `MyBinaryModule` (as shown in the following screenshot), or whatever you like.

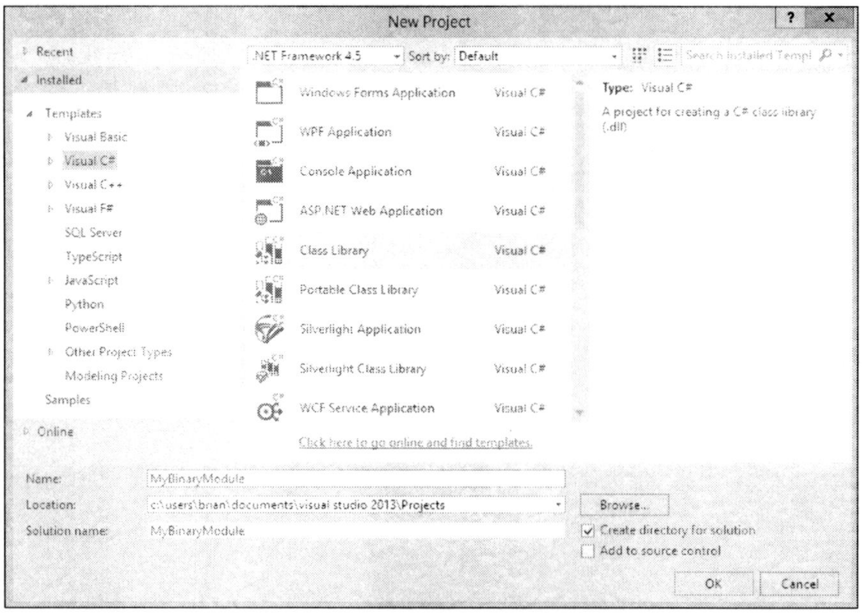

Then, add a reference to the root namespace for Windows PowerShell, the `System.Management.Automation` namespace.

> The `System.Management.Automation` DLL file can be found by navigating to **C:** | **Windows** | **Assembly** | **GAC_MSIL** | **System.Management.Automation** | **1.0.0.0__31bf3856ad364e35**.

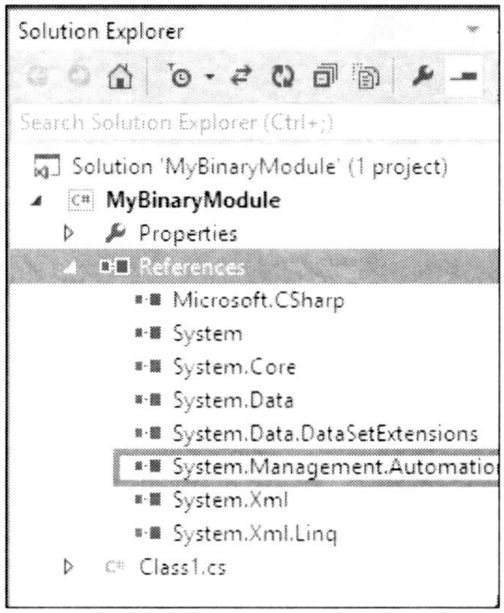

By now, everything should be ready to write your cmdlets using a normal C# code. In order to identify your class as a PowerShell cmdlet class, use the `[Cmdlet()]` attribute in your class. The cmdlet attribute is the cmdlet's name that is composed of two parts: verb and noun. Also, the cmdlet class should be derived from the base class called `Cmdlet`. This class provides three virtual methods that are called by the runtime. These methods are `BeginProcessing()`, `ProcessRecord()`, and `EndProcessing() Cmdlets must override at least one of these methods to process records.`

```
[Cmdlet(VerbsCommon.Get,"EvenOrOdd")]
    public class EvenorOdd: Cmdlet
    {
protected override void ProcessRecord()
      {
        base.ProcessRecord();
      }
    }
```

You can also define a parameter to the cmdlet using the `[Parameter()]` attribute within the class.

```
[Parameter(Position = 0,
            ValueFromPipeline = true,
            ValueFromPipelineByPropertyName = true,
            HelpMessage = @"The range of numbers to be checked")]
        public int[] Numbers
        {
            get { return num; }
            set { num = value; }
        }
        private int[] num;
```

You can use one of the `[Validate*()]` attributes above the `[Parameter()]` attribute to validate the arguments for this parameter. For example, you can specify a set of three possible values for the `PersonName` parameter:

```
[ValidateSet("Gates", "Jobs", "Ballmer")]
[Parameter(Position = 0, Mandatory = true)]
public string PersonName
{
get { return personName; }
set { personName = value; }
}
private string personName;
```

Moreover, you can use the `WriteVerbose()` and `WriteDebug()` methods to display debugging information during the cmdlet execution using the `-Verbose` and `-Debug` switches. Also, we use the `WriteObject()` method to return the execution output of the cmdlet.

> Read more about the root namespace for Windows PowerShell at `http://msdn.microsoft.com/en-us/library/System.Management.Automation(v=vs.85).aspx`.

After finishing your code, the final cmdlet class should look like the following screenshot:

```
[Cmdlet("Validate", "EmailAddress")]
0 references
public class RemoveBadWords : Cmdlet
{
    [Parameter(Position = 0,
       ValueFromPipeline = true,
       ValueFromPipelineByPropertyName = true,
       HelpMessage = @"The E-mail address to validate")]
    3 references
    public string EmailAddress
    {
        get { return Email; }
        set { Email = value; }
    }
    private string Email;

    1 reference
    protected override void ProcessRecord()
    {
        base.ProcessRecord();

        //Write Verbose information to be displayed by -Verbose
        WriteVerbose("Validating Email Address: " + EmailAddress);

        //Write Verbose information to be displayed by -Debug
        WriteDebug("Validating Email Address: " + EmailAddress);

        Regex reg = new Regex(@"(\w+@[a-zA-Z_]+?\.[a-zA-Z]{2,6})");

        //Write Object information to be displayed as a result of cmdlet execu
        WriteObject(reg.IsMatch(EmailAddress));
```

Now, it is the time to compile the project to build it into a binary module. In Visual Studio, go to **Build | Build Solution**. There is a `MyBinaryModule.dll` file in the `bin/debug` subdirectory of the project directory.

Congratulations, you have just created your first binary module. Now open the PowerShell console and use the `Import-Module` cmdlet to import it.

```
PS C:\> Import-Module Import-Module "D:\MyBinaryModule\MyBinaryModule.
dll"

PS C:\> Get-Command -Module MyBinaryModule | Select CommandType, Name

CommandType   Name
-----------   ----
     Cmdlet   Get-EvenOrOdd
     Cmdlet   Validate-EmailAddress

#Using Validate-EmailAddress cmdlet
```

```
PS C:\ > Validate-EmailAddress -EmailAddress sherif@xyz -Verbose
VERBOSE: Validating Email Address: sherif@xyz
False

PS C:\ > Validate-EmailAddress -EmailAddress sherif@xyz.com
True

#Using Get-EvenOrOdd cmdlet
PS C:\Users\v-shta> Get-EvenOrOdd -Numbers @(2,5,13,17,24,33)
2 is even
5 is odd
13 is odd
(...)
```

The manifest modules

A manifest module is the module that has a PowerShell data file, `-manifest-` (`.psd1`), which describes its components and contents, and how this module will be processed. The manifest module file can include one or more nested script modules or binary modules.

The manifest is a text file that has information about the module itself such as author, company, description, files to include, assemblies to load, minimum PowerShell version, and minimum .NET framework version. Usually, the manifest file is not required by modules unless you want to export an assembly installed in the global assembly cache, use the updatable help feature, or set certain restrictions.

To create a module manifest, we use the `New-ModuleManifest` cmdlet to build an empty manifest module template that can be modified later using any text editor. Also, you can define the manifest information during template creation using the different parameters available with the `New-ModuleManifest` cmdlet.

```
New-ModuleManifest -Author "Sherif Talaat" -CompanyName "Packt
Publishing" -ModuleVersion "1.0" -ProcessorArchitecture Amd64
-PowerShellVersion "3.0" -PowerShellHostName "ConsoleHost, Windows
PowerShell ISE Host" -Description "my first module manifest" -FileList
"myScriptModule.psm1" -ModuletoProcess "Bitlocker" -Path "D:\Modules\
myScriptModule\myScriptModule.psd1"
```

The following screenshot shows a sample of a module manifest file:

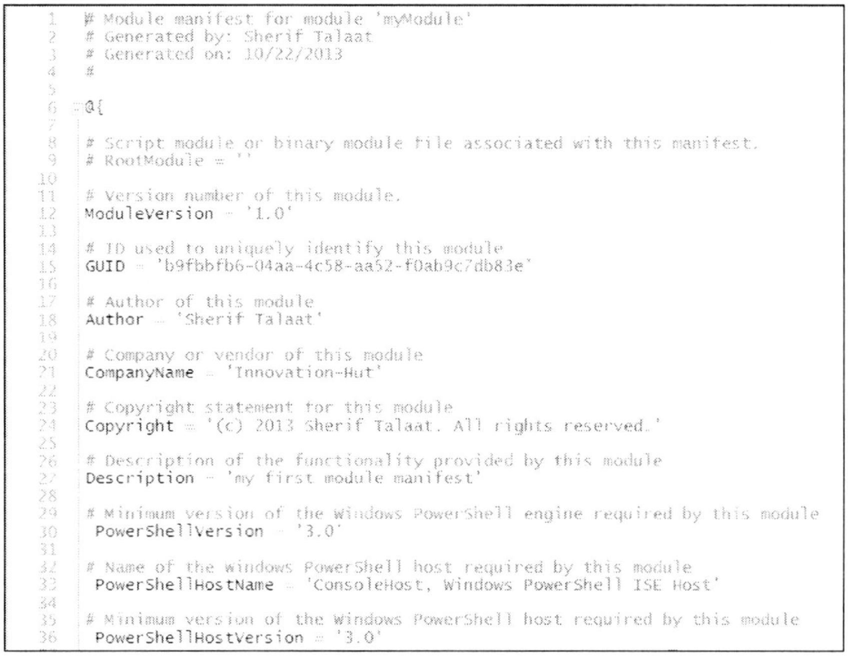

```
# Module manifest for module 'myModule'
# Generated by: Sherif Talaat
# Generated on: 10/22/2013
#

@{

# Script module or binary module file associated with this manifest.
# RootModule = ''

# Version number of this module.
ModuleVersion = '1.0'

# ID used to uniquely identify this module
GUID = 'b9fbbfb6-04aa-4c58-aa52-f0ab9c7db83e'

# Author of this module
Author = 'Sherif Talaat'

# Company or vendor of this module
CompanyName = 'Innovation-Hut'

# Copyright statement for this module
Copyright = '(c) 2013 Sherif Talaat. All rights reserved.'

# Description of the functionality provided by this module
Description = 'my first module manifest'

# Minimum version of the Windows PowerShell engine required by this module
 PowerShellVersion = '3.0'

# Name of the windows PowerShell host required by this module
 PowerShellHostName = 'ConsoleHost, Windows PowerShell ISE Host'

# Minimum version of the Windows PowerShell host required by this module
 PowerShellHostVersion = '3.0'
```

The dynamic modules

A dynamic module is a module that does not persist on the disk but in the memory and will be lost once you close your PowerShell session. These types of modules can be created from functions and scriptblocks within the same session, which is useful to developers for better object-oriented scripting, and also to administrators when you want to execute certain modules on remote computers using PowerShell remoting where these modules physically exist.

The dynamic modules are being created using the `New-Module` cmdlet with parameters such as `-Function` and `-ScriptBlock` that specify which function and scriptblocks are to be included in this module.

```
#Create a dynamic module with single function
PS C:\> New-Module -ScriptBlock {Function Send-Greetings($name){"Good
Morning, $name"}}

#Trigger a function
PS C:\> Send-Greetings -name Sherif
Good Morning, Sherif
```

Script debugging and error handling

In the previous chapter, we mentioned that PowerShell supports script debugging for both local and remote scripts. The debugging feature in PowerShell is like that in other programming languages. It allows you to toggle breakpoints, step into, step out, step over, and even call the stack. The script debugging is available in the PowerShell console host via cmdlets and in PowerShell ISE via GUI and cmdlets.

The debugging feature in PowerShell ISE is available under the **Debug** tab, as shown in the following screenshot:

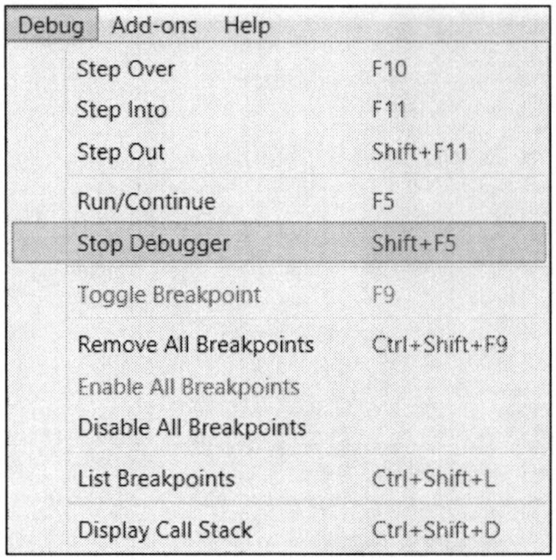

Windows PowerShell also provides a set of cmdlets that allow you to perform a debugging operation via commands without using any GUI. These cmdlets are very helpful when you are using Windows Server Core where PowerShell ISE is not available. The cmdlets are all about managing the breakpoints in your scripts.

```
PS C:\ > Get-Command -Name *Breakpoint | Select Name
Name
----
Disable-PSBreakpoint
Enable-PSBreakpoint
Get-PSBreakpoint
Remove-PSBreakpoint
Set-PSBreakpoint
```

In addition to the `PSBreakpoint` cmdlets, you also have a few other commands available during the debugging mode only for the other debugging operations.

Working with breakpoints

A breakpoint is the designated spot in your code where the execution operation pauses to start the debugging mode. Windows PowerShell has three different types of breakpoints that can be used within your scripts and can be toggled using the `Set-PSBreakpoint` cmdlet.

- **Line breakpoint**: The script pauses when the designated line is reached. It is toggled by defining the line number using the `-Line` switch.

  ```
  PS C:\> Set-PSBreakpoint -script c:\myscript.ps1 -Line 7
  ```

- **Variable breakpoint**: The script pauses whenever the designated variable's value is changed. It is toggled by defining the variable name without the `$` prefix using the `-Variable` switch.

  ```
  PS C:\> Set-PSBreakpoint -script c:\myscript.ps1 -Variable
  Services
  ```

- **Command breakpoint**: The script pauses whenever the designated command is about to run. The command can be a cmdlet or the name of a function you created. It is toggled by defining the command name using the `-Command` switch.

  ```
  PS C:\> Set-PSBreakpoint -script c:\myscript.ps1 -Command Get-
  Process
  ```

Now, we have defined three different breakpoints on a script. Use the `Get-PSBreakpoint` cmdlet to list all the breakpoints you have in a script.

```
PS C:\> Get-PSBreakpoint -Script myscript.ps1
ID Script                  Line Command      Variable
  -- ------                ---- -------      --------
  11 myscript.ps1          7
  12 myscript.ps1                            Services
  13 myscript.ps1               Get-Process
```

You can also use the `Remove-PSBreakpoint` cmdlet to permanently remove a breakpoint or use the `Disable-PSBreakpoint` cmdlet to temporarily disable a breakpoint, and you can enable it back again using the `Enable-PSBreakpoint` cmdlet.

```
#Disable Variable breakpoint services
Get-PSBreakpoint -Variable Services | Disable-PSBreakpoint

#Enable Variable breakpoint services
Get-PSBreakpoint -Variable Services | Enable-PSBreakpoint

#Remove Variable breakpoint services
Get-PSBreakpoint -Variable Services | Remove-PSBreakpoint
```

Debugging your script

Once you define the breakpoints, you can execute your script normally. Whenever the first designated breakpoint is reached, a message will appear to inform you that execution operation has hit a breakpoint. Then, you will find that **[DBG]:** continually appears as a prefix for every command before **PS C:\>>** to indicate that you are working in debugging mode until you stop the debugger using *Shift* + *F5*.

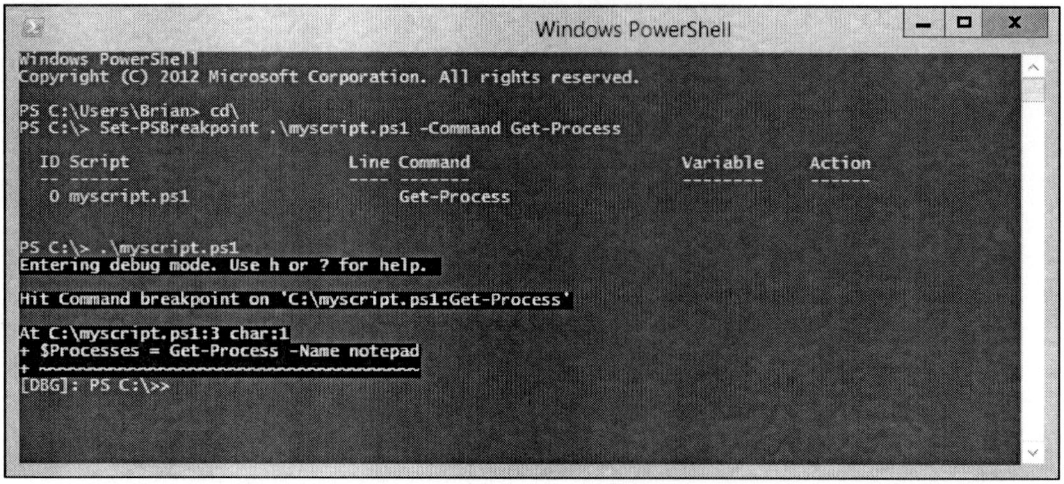

While in debugging mode, you can use the commands in the following table to perform normal debugging operations:

Debugging task	Command	Shortcut
Step into	`StepInto`	*S*
Step out	`StepOut`	*O*
Step over	`StepOver`	*V*
Continue	`Continue`	*C*
List	`List`	*L*
Stop	`Quit`	*Q*
Call stack	`Get-PSCallStack`	*K*

Previously, script debugging in Windows PowerShell was limited to scripts running on the local machine. If you tried to set script breakpoints in a remote session, it would trigger an error. In Windows PowerShell 4.0, you can set breakpoints in remote sessions and debug remote running scripts from the console in the same way as you debug local running scripts. In order to use the remote script debugging feature, you must have Windows PowerShell 4.0 on local and remote machines.

Error-handling techniques

Windows PowerShell uses the `Try{}`, `Catch{}`, `Finally{}` statements as in C# to handle terminating errors (exceptions). The terminating error will not be handled by the `Catch{}` statement until you change the value of the `$ErrorActionPreference` variable to `stop`.

```
$ErrorActionPreference = "stop"

Try
{
    Get-ChildItem C:\movies
}
Catch [System.Exception]
{
    "Item not found"
}
Finally
{
    New-item -ItemType Directory -Path C:\Movies
    "Item has been created"
}
```

> You can read more about the `Try/Catch/Finally` statements and the other error-handling techniques in the following **About** topics:
>
> - **About_Trap**
> - **About_Throw**
> - **About_Try_Catch_Finally**

The $Error and $LastExistCode variables

Whenever an error occurs in PowerShell during execution, it will be logged in a global variable `$Error`. This variable is an `ArrayList` instance of PowerShell error objects where the most recent error is stored at index zero. You can get more details about the error record by manipulating the `$Error` variable as shown in the following snippet:

```
PS D:\> $Error[0].Exception
Cannot find path 'C:\movies' because it does not exist.

PS D:\> $Error[0].FullyQualifiedErrorId
PathNotFound,Microsoft.PowerShell.Commands.GetChildItemCommand

PS D:\> $Error[0].ScriptStackTrace
at <ScriptBlock>, <No file>: line 5
```

> You can read more about the error record information at http://msdn.microsoft.com/en-us/library/system.management.automation.errorrecord_members(v=vs.85).aspx.

The exit code is used to determine the execution status for native applications such as `ping.exe` or `robocopy.exe` whether they are completed successfully or not. Usually, it uses `0` to identify successes and `1` for failures, but sometimes some applications use a wide range of exit codes to determine different types of errors. Anyway, PowerShell is using the `$LastExitCode` variable to log the exit code information for the native applications and external processes.

Building GUI with PowerShell

We have spoken enough about Windows PowerShell with .NET framework and how it leverages .NET framework capabilities to do many useful tasks. The last thing to mention in this chapter is how PowerShell can use the underlying .NET framework to build a GUI.

The following PowerShell code demonstrates how to use the regular .NET framework namespace to build a simple WPF form with a single button:

```
$form = new-object Windows.Forms.Form
$form.Text = "Main Form"

$button = new-object Windows.Forms.Button
$button.text="Close Me!"
$button.Dock="fill"
$button.add_click({$form.close()})

$form.controls.add($button)
$form.Add_Shown({$form.Activate()})
$form.ShowDialog()
```

The previous code will create the form illustrated in the following screenshot. Very nice, huh?

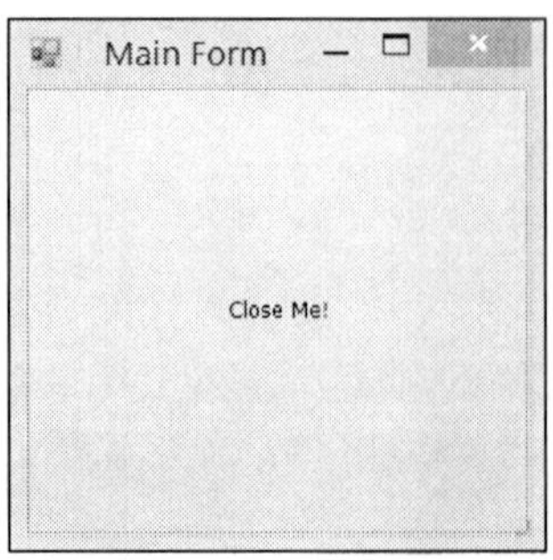

Although you can build whatever forms and controls you want, you still have to write hundreds of lines of code. For this reason, you can use one of PowerShell's third-party tools that provides a GUI designer for PowerShell such as **SAPIEN PowerShell Studio**.

Summary

In this chapter, we learned how to use Windows PowerShell to work closely with WMI, COM, and XML. We also learned what CIM is and how to use it via PowerShell. In addition, we shined a light on working with .NET objects and how to use .NET to extend Windows PowerShell capabilities.

Also, we learned what modules are, the different types of modules, and how to create a module that can be used to automate our own custom-developed applications. Finally, we jumped into script-debugging and error-handling techniques in PowerShell.

In the next chapter, we will learn how to use PowerShell to perform different administration tasks that we might face on a daily basis, such as preparing application requirements, handling user and group permissions, managing and configuring IIS, and maintaining SQL Server databases.

3

PowerShell for Your Daily Administration Tasks

In the Information Technology field, there is no black or white, but many shades of gray, starting with white and ending with black. This means that irrespective of whether you're an IT professional or a developer, you must have a good knowledge of the other side of the coin. If you are an IT professional or a system administrator, you should have good programming and scripting skills that allow you to do your tasks in a more efficient and productive way. If you are a developer, you should have a good knowledge about networking, security, different platforms, and so on, in order to understand the system you are developing on and for the system you are developing.

For developers, you sometimes have to wear the IT professional's hat when it comes to preparing a server for your application, installing the required software components, upgrading your software, and so on. It's very common to find yourself as a developer preparing a web server, maintaining a database server, troubleshooting the operating system's error, and many other administration tasks to perform on a daily basis, which is another good reason to use Windows PowerShell to make your life easier.

This chapter will focus on using Windows PowerShell with different products and technologies that you might/already use on a daily basis in the form of a set of real scenarios and examples.

In this chapter, we will cover:

- Understanding and working PowerShell remoting
- Building and using PowerShell workflows
- Working with Windows roles and features
- Managing Windows users and groups
- Working with **Internet Information Services** (**IIS**)
- Working with SQL Server

Windows PowerShell remoting

PowerShell remoting is one of the most powerful and impressive capabilities of Windows PowerShell. The remoting feature has been introduced in PowerShell Version 2. This feature uses **Windows Remote Management** (**WinRM**) to connect to any remote computer that is not physically accessible within your location, or even in a different geographic location. To make it simple, it is all about using the PowerShell console on your local machine to manage and control remote computers in different locations.

On Windows Server 2012 and 2012 R2, PowerShell remoting is enabled by default. However, you can use the `Enable-PSRemoting` cmdlet to enable it on an older server version and on Windows clients as well. You might also use the `-SkipNetworkProfileCheck` switch to allow remoting on public network profiles.

```
PS C:\> Enable-PSRemoting -Force -SkipNetworkProfileCheck
```

The `Enable-PSRemoting` cmdlet configures the computer to receive and accept PowerShell remote commands. What this command does is configure the WinRM service, creates listeners to accept the request, opens firewall ports and allows exceptions, registers PowerShell sessions, and changes the security descriptor to allow remote access. Of course, at any point, you can use the `Disable-PSRemoting` cmdlet to disable it.

Four different ways of using remoting

There are four different modes, usages, ways, or whatever you name it, to use the PowerShell remoting.

Interactive remoting

The first method is the interactive mode. In this mode, we use the `Enter-PSSession` cmdlet along with the `-ComputerName` switch to connect to the remote computer.

```
PS C:\> Enter-PSSession -ComputerName Sherif-PC
```

Once you connect successfully to your target machine, the prompt will be changed, and you can have the target computer's name at the beginning of the line, as shown in the following screenshot:

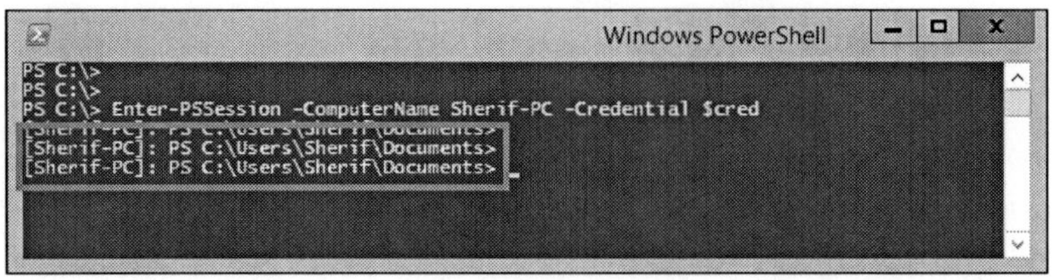

In this mode, you can execute whatever commands you want, as if you are using the local PowerShell console on the remote computer. For example, try to run the `Get-Process` cmdlet or even a native command such as `ipconfig.exe` and see what results you will get. You can close the remote session and return back to your local machine by using the `Exit-PSSession` cmdlet.

Ad hoc remoting

Some PowerShell cmdlets support remoting by design. For example, a cmdlet such as `Get-Service` or `Get-Process` has the `-ComputerName` parameter. What happens here is that you specify one or more computers using this parameter, and during the execution of the command Windows PowerShell will connect to each computer, open a session, execute the commands, get the output, and finally close the session.

This method looks fine when you want to run a quick command on-the-fly, but it is definitely not the best candidate when it comes to performance and efficiency.

Persistent session

This mode is a little bit similar to ad hoc remoting style, but more efficient. The trick here is creating a persistent remoting session that remains connected and active by using the `New-PSSession` cmdlet as shown in the following code. Thus, if you want to run a group of commands on a computer, you do not have to open a session for each command as in the case of ad hoc remoting.

```
#create new PowerShell session
PS C:\>  $s = New-PSSession -ComputerName 192.168.1.2

#Use the session by Invoke-Command
PS C:\> Invoke-Command -Session $s -FilePath D:\myScript.ps1
```

The persistent sessions are robust and resilient. This means that you can disconnect your session using the `Disconnect-PSSession` cmdlet without affecting the running operation. You can also connect to the same session again from the same computer or even from a different computer to continue your previous work as if you are using an RDP session. To connect again to a disconnected session, use the `Connect-PSSession` cmdlet. Last but not least, whenever you finish your work, make sure to remove the unwanted sessions using the `Remove-PSSession` cmdlet.

Implicit remoting

Implicit remoting is simply importing the cmdlets from the remote computer, which you do not have on your local machine. Thus, you do not have to install an extra module or register more snap-ins. Let's elaborate more with an example: you have a server running SQL Server 2012 and you want to manage this server using PowerShell. So, instead of installing the SQL Server PowerShell module on the local machine, you open a remote PowerShell session on the SQL Server machine, load the SQL module in the remote session, and then import the SQL cmdlets to your local session.

```
PS C:\> $s = New-PSSession -ComputerName SQL-01
PS C:\> Invoke-Command -Session $s -ScriptBlock {Import-Module SQLPS}
```

Now, we have a session, `$s`, which has all the cmdlets loaded by default in addition to the SQL module cmdlets. You use the `Import-PSSession` cmdlet to import all these commands on a temporary module on your local machine, or you can export a specific command in a persistent module using the `Export-PSSession` cmdlet, and then import it.

```
#Import session to temp module
PS C:\> Import-PSSession -Session $s -Prefix Remote -AllowClobber

#Export session to persistent module
PS C:\> Export-PSSession -Session $s -CommandName *SQL* -Module SQLPS
-OutputModule SQL01Cmdlets
PS C:\> Import-Module SQL01Cmdlets
```

The `Import-PSSession` cmdlet has two important switches:

- `AllowClobber`: This allows the cmdlets with the same name as local cmdlets to be imported
- `Prefix`: This adds a prefix to the noun of each imported cmdlet to easily identify it and to avoid a conflict in case there are two commands with the same name

The implicit remoting technique is already being used by a few Microsoft products, of which the most popular is Microsoft Exchange Server. In this, you open a session to exchange a virtual directory that has all the configuration and cmdlets, and then import it to your local session.

```
#Create new implicit remoting session
$Session = New-PSSession -ConfigurationName Microsoft.Exchange
-ConnectionUri "http://Exch.Contoso.local/PowerShell" -Credential
(Get-Credential) -Authentication Kerberos

#Import the PowerShell remoting Session
Import-PSSession -Session $Session
```

Windows PowerShell Workflow (PSW)

A workflow represents a set of objects, tasks, and activities that are connected together and running concurrently or sequentially, or even both. In an IT world, the word "workflow" is always associated with another word called automation. For example, in Microsoft SharePoint Server, we use workflows to automate approval processes such as a vacation request approval, and in **Microsoft Forefront Identity Management** (**FIM**), we use workflows to reset users' passwords, and a lot of other examples in many other applications and technologies.

Workflow capabilities have been introduced in Windows PowerShell 3.0, and it is designed specifically to help you perform long-time and effort-consuming complex tasks across multiple and different devices in different locations.

You might wonder about the real value of Windows PowerShell Workflows. You already use PowerShell to write different scripts and modules that allow you to perform long-running tasks, and this is the aim of scripting in general. Well, before I tell you the answer, let's think about these questions together: can you write a script that can restart a device and wait for this device to boot up to resume the rest of the commands again? Can you write a single script that runs on multiple devices concurrently? PowerShell Workflows have been designed to be fit in scenarios such as:

- Executing long-running and repeatable activities
- Running activities in parallel across one or more computers
- Interruptible, stoppable, restartable, and even parallelizable activities

In Windows PowerShell, a script consists of a set of commands; however, a workflow consists of a set of activities. The commands normally represent actions you want to execute, but the activities represent tasks you want to perform. Moreover, commands are being executed sequentially; however, activities can be executed sequentially and concurrently.

There are two methods to define a workflow: either by using PowerShell syntax, or since it is built on top of **Windows Workflow Foundation** (**WF**) you can use an XAML file designed by Visual Studio Workflow Designer.

> Read about creating Windows PowerShell Workflows using Microsoft Visual Studio at `http://msdn.microsoft.com/en-us/library/windows/desktop/hh852738(v=vs.85).aspx`.

Creating a workflow using PowerShell

Writing a PowerShell workflow is similar to writing a PowerShell function with a little difference. The first difference is using the keyword `Workflow` instead of `Function`.

```
Workflow Send-Greetings
{
  "Hello World..!!"
}
PS C:\> Send-Greetings
Hello World..!!
```

The parameters' definition is similar to functions using the `param( )` attribute, and you can also use `[CmdletBinding()]` to add some advanced workflow features. The `CmdletBinding` attribute allows you to add advanced capabilities to your function and workflows, such as adding the `-Verbose`, `-Debug`, `-whatif`, and `-confirm` parameters to your workflow without implementing them manually. It also defines the HelpUri that will be used by the `Get-Help` cmdlets to get online help for the workflow or function. You can refer to the conceptual help topic *about_Functions_Advanced_Parameters* for more information about the cmdlet's binding parameters.

```
Workflow Send-Greetings
{
  [CmdletBinding()]
  Param([string] $Name)
  "Hello, $Name"
}
C:\> Send-Greetings -Name Sherif
Hello, Sherif
```

Executing a PowerShell Workflow

PowerShell workflows can be executed concurrently and/or sequentially by using the keywords: `Parallel` and `Sequence`.

Sequential execution

By design, the activities in PowerShell are executed sequentially unless you change this behavior. They are executed similar to functions where each command should finish its execution before jumping to the next, and so on, till the end of the code. The following code is a very simple workflow that gets the list of services and processes running on a computer:

```
Workflow Get-Information
{
```

```
    Get-Service
    Get-Process
    Get-CimClass -ClassName Win32_BIOS
}
```

Run the previous code on your machine and watch the output. You will notice that the services' information will be displayed first, then the processes', and finally the BIOS's information.

In some cases, you might want to run a set of activities sequentially within a parallel execution block. To do that, use the keyword `Sequence` as shown in the following code block:

```
Workflow Test-Workflow
{
  Sequence
  {
    <Activity_1>
    <Activity_2>
    <Activity_3>
  }
}
```

Sequence execution is useful for defining a set of activities to run sequentially inside a `Parallel` or `ForEach -Parallel` execution.

Parallel execution

One of the advantages of PowerShell workflows is the ability to execute a set of activities concurrently. This way of execution is called parallel execution. To define activities to be executed concurrently, use the keyword `Parallel`. Let's use the same example we used in the previous section, but execute commands in parallel this time.

```
Workflow Get-Information
{
  Parallel
  {
    Get-Service
    Get-Process
    Get-CimClass -ClassName Win32_BIOS
  }
}
```

Again, run the previous code on your machine and watch the output. This time you will notice that the outputs of these commands are being displayed randomly without any order. Each time you run this workflow, you will receive a totally different order.

Parallel execution is also available with the `ForEach` loop. The `ForEach -Parallel` loop is a combination of `Sequence` and `Parallel` executions. The `ForEach -Parallel` loop will execute activities sequentially on the items in the collection in parallel. For example, if there is a collection of computers where a set of activities such as joining this computer to a domain is being executed, this activity will be executed in sequence on all the computers at the same time.

```
Workflow Test-Workflow
{
  $Computers = Get-Content C:\list.txt

ForEach -Parallel ($comp in $Computers)
{
Add-Computer -ComputerName $comp -LocalCredential Server01\Admin01
  -DomainName contoso.local -Credential contoso\Admin02
}
```

Parallel execution is useful for running independent activities concurrently, such as starting a process and restarting a service at the same time, where each activity is running independent of the other one.

InlineScript activity

As mentioned earlier, PowerShell workflows use activities, which means that the normal PowerShell cmdlets cannot be used in a workflow. To make life easier, the PowerShell team has already implemented activities equivalent to most of PowerShell's core cmdlets, so you can use them with the same name without getting confused. For example, the `Get-Service` cmdlet is different from the `Get-Service` activity; the former is used in PowerShell scripts, and the latter is used in PowerShell workflows.

> The list of cmdlets that have no equivalent activities is available at:
> `http://technet.microsoft.com/en-us/library/jj574194.aspx`

In order to use the PowerShell cmdlets inside a workflow, use the `inlineScript` activity. It's a special activity that allows the execution of any PowerShell command that is valid in PowerShell but not supported by workflows, for example, executing the `*.ps1` file or calling a dynamic parameter inside a workflow.

Let's elaborate more; if you tried to use the `GetType()` method within a workflow, you will get the following error:

```
Method invocation is not supported in a Windows PowerShell
  Workflow. To use .NET scripting, place your commands in an
  inline script: InlineScript { <commands> }.
```

To get over this error, use the `GetType()` method within your workflow. Then, use the `inlineScript` activity as shown in the following code:

```
Workflow UseInlineScript
{
  InlineScript{ (Get-Date).GetType() }
}
PS C:\> UseInlineScript
Public    IsSerial Name             BaseType             PSComputerName
------  -------- ----             --------             --------------
True    True     DateTime         System.ValueType     localhost
```

Controlling the PowerShell workflow execution

One of the most interesting features in PowerShell workflow and what makes it unique over a normal script is the flexibility of controlling the execution; at any point, you can interrupt, suspend, and resume the workflow execution; you can even restart the computer while running the workflow and complete the execution upon startup.

You can suspend the workflow execution using the `Suspend-Workflow` activity, which will save the execution state, variables, and values in a checkpoint and return the job ID for the suspended workflow. So, you can use the job ID as a parameter for the `Resume-Job` cmdlet to resume the workflow execution again.

In the following example, we will learn how to suspend and resume the workflow execution:

```
Workflow Test-Workflow
{
  Get-Service
  Suspend-Workflow
  Get-Process
}
```

Once you run the workflow, the first two activities will be executed and the workflow will be suspended, and the result of `Suspend-Workflow` will give information about the workflow's executed job.

```
HasMoreData       : True
StatusMessage     :
Location          : localhost
Command           : Test-Workflow
JobStateInfo      : Suspended
Finished          : System.Threading.ManualResetEvent
InstanceId        : 3bbd1e36-2683-42b2-a2ca-74e08512abca
Id                : 34
Name              : Job34
ChildJobs         : {Job35}
PSBeginTime       : 12/20/2013 1:12:56 PM
PSEndTime         : 12/20/2013 1:12:57 PM
PSJobTypeName     : PSWorkflowJob
State             : Suspended
(...)
```

In order to resume the workflow again, use the `Resume-Job` cmdlet with the job name mentioned in the previous output.

```
PS C:\>Resume-Job -Name Job34
```

In order to get the results of the activities executed after resuming, in our case `Get-Process`, we will use the `Get-Job` and `Receive-Job` cmdlets.

```
PS C:\>Get-Job -Name Job34 | Receive-Job
```

As PowerShell workflow is recoverable, you can restart the target computer and smoothly resume the workflow again using the `Restart-Computer` activity. Simply use the switch `-wait` with `Restart-Computer`. So, the workflow will wait for the computer to restart and reconnect again before proceeding with the workflow's execution.

In this example, the workflow will restart the targeted computer after executing `Activity 1` and `Activity 2`, and then wait for the computer to boot up again to resume and execute `Activity 3`. You can also use the `-PSConnectionRetryCount` and `-PSConnectionRetryInterval` parameters to specify the connection retries and the interval between each connection's retry.

```
Workflow Test-Workflow
{
  <Activity_1>
  <Activity_2>
```

```
    Restart-Computer -Wait -PSConnectionRetryInterval 4 -
    PSConnectionRetryCount 8
    <Activity_3>
}
```

Persistent workflows

In order to maintain the previous features of the PowerShell workflow, it is a must to implement another feature in workflows, which is checkpoints. The checkpoints in a PowerShell Workflow take a snapshot of the current state and data, and then save it in the profile of a user who is executing this workflow on the hard disk. Thus, when resumed, the workflow will start from the last checkpoint instead of starting from the beginning. PowerShell, by default, adds checkpoints in the beginning and ending of the workflow. In addition, you can use the `-PSPersist` switch with any activity to take a checkpoint after completing the execution of it. Also, you can use the `Checkpoint-Workflow` activity at any point in your flow to take a checkpoint.

The following command will show you how to use the `-PSPersist` switch:

```
PS C:\>Test-Workflow -PSPersist $True
```

Workflows are used to execute tasks faster, so using checkpoints without need or optimization will slow the execution and make it useless.

In case of using pipelines and parallel executions, checkpoints will not be taken until the completion of pipeline or parallel activities; however, you can use the checkpoint in sequence activities to take a checkpoint after completion of every single activity.

Windows PowerShell in action

In this section, we will go on a tour to discover how PowerShell is being used in many different products and technologies, such as Windows Server, SQL Server, and IIS.

Working with Windows roles and features

Managing Windows roles and features is one of the most important basic and repetitive tasks while dealing with a server operating system, such as Windows Server.

In Windows Server, you can manage roles and features using the PowerShell Server Manager module. This module allows listing, adding, and removing roles or features via three cmdlets: `Get-WindowsFeature`, `Install-WindowsFeature`, and `Uninstall-WindowsFeature`.

The following example shows how to use the `Get-WindowsFeature` cmdlet to list all the installed roles and features on a local server:

```
#Get list of all installed Roles and Features
PS C:\> Get-WindowsFeature | where Installed -eq $true
```

Refer to the following screenshot for roles and features:

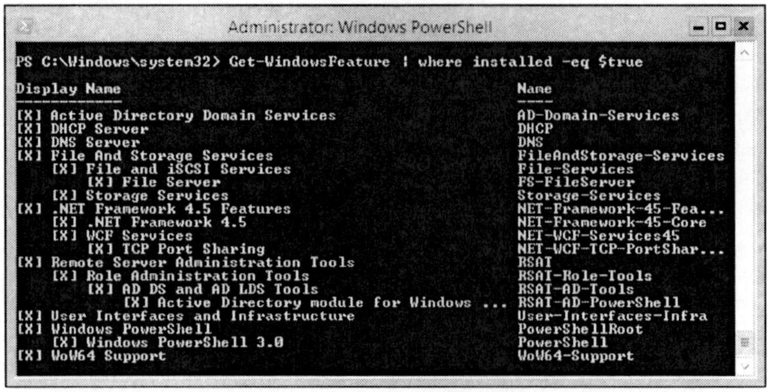

Working with Windows features using PowerShell is very useful even if you have the luxury of a GUI, especially when you want to install a set of prerequisites for something such as SharePoint Server or SQL Server on one or more servers.

Installing Windows roles and features

For the purpose of installing a Windows role or feature, you will use the `Install-WindowsFeature` cmdlet that comes with a couple of very interesting parameters, which are as follows:

- `IncludeAllSubFeature`: This is used to install a role or feature that has multiple subfeatures where you want to install all of them in one step. It's a good candidate for roles such as Web Server, File Server, and RSAT.
- `IncludeManagementTools`: This is used when you install a role or feature using PowerShell. It will install the role itself without the management console. So, this switch will ensure that you will get the management interface installed automatically alongside your component.

The following example demonstrates how to use the `Install-WindowsFeature` cmdlet to install IIS (Web Server role) with all subfeatures along with the management console:

```
#Installing IIS Role using Install-WindowsFeature cmdlet
PS C:\> Install-WindowsFeature Web-Server -IncludeAllSubFeature -
  IncludeManagementTools
```

You can also use this cmdlet to install a role or feature on multiple remote computers at the same time using the `-ComputerName` parameter.

```
#Installing IIS Role on multiple servers
PS C:\> 'WebSrv01','WebSrv02','WebSrv03' | Foreach-Object {
   Install-WindowsFeature Web-Server -IncludeAllSubFeature -
IncludeManagementTools -ComputerName $_ }
```

If you want to install a role or feature on a remote computer that uses a different credential than your credentials, then you have the option to provide the remote computers' credential using the `-Credential` parameter.

```
#Installing IIS on multiple servers using different credentials
PS C:\> $cred = Get-Credential mylab.local\Administrator
PS C:\> 'WebSrv01','WebSrv02','WebSrv03' | Foreach-Object {
   Install-WindowsFeature Web-Server -IncludeAllSubFeature -
IncludeManagementTools -ComputerName $_  -Credential $cred}
```

You can also use the `-ConfigurationFilePath` parameter to install the roles and features specified in the xml configuration file generated by the **Add Roles and Features Wizard** in the **Server Manager** consoles as shown in the following screenshot and the code:

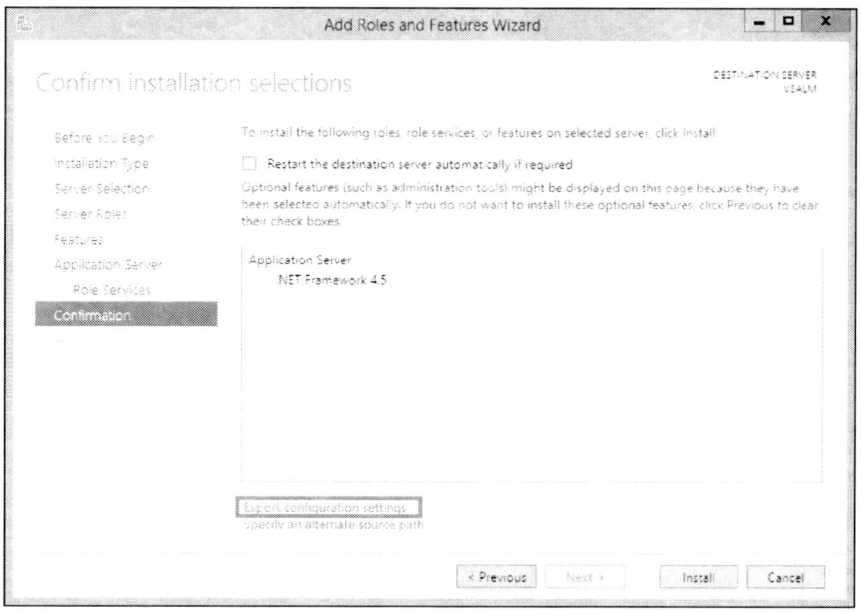


```
#Install features from a previously generated Config file
PS C:\> Install-WindowsFeature -ConfigurationFilePath d:\
WebServerConfigFile.xml
```

Last but not least, if you have an offline **virtual hard disk** (**VHD**) for a HyperV file, you can use the `-vhd` parameter to install Windows roles and features on it after it has been mounted using the **Deployment Image Servicing and Management** (**DISM**) tools.

Uninstalling Windows roles and features

The process of removing roles and features is very similar to that of installing them. For the purpose of uninstalling a Windows role or feature, you use the `Uninstall-WindowsFeature` cmdlet. Actually, it is the opposite operation, but we are using almost the exact parameters, such as in the `Install-WindowsFeature` cmdlet; however, there is no `-IncludeAllSubFeature` parameter because once you uninstall a parent role or feature, it will automatically uninstall all of its subfeatures.

Also, here is a new parameter, `-Remove`, that can be used to delete the role's and the feature's physical files stored under the `Windows\WinSxS` directory.

> You can use the `Get-WindowsOptionalFeature`, `Enable-WindowsOptionalFeature`, and `Disable-WindowsOptioanlFeature` cmdlets that come as part of the `DISM` module to manage the optional features of Windows' client operating systems such as Windows 8 or 8.1.

Managing local users and groups

Usually, working with users and groups used to be a task purely related to system administration. Although this is totally true when it comes to managing domain users and groups as part of managing the domain environment, when it comes to local users and groups, sometimes you, as a developer, find yourself dealing with local users and groups. In some cases, you need to do something like granting administrative rights to a development account, managing access to your web application, configuring **SQL Server Reporting Services** (**SSRS**), and a lot of other similar tasks, so that PowerShell can help you in automating such tasks without even repeating them each and every time. Simply build a script with your own settings and configuration, then use it whenever you want to save your time and effort.

If you had the chance to develop an application using C# that works with users and groups, then you definitely know that the `DirectoryServices` class is your hero for managing users and groups. This means that you are still able to follow the same way in PowerShell by creating a .NET object of this class, and then manipulating this object as if you are working with a normal .NET-managed code. Although this might make you feel that you are in your comfort zone, this will cost you a lot of time and effort. On the other hand, PowerShell provides you with an **Active Directory Services Interface** (**ADSI**) type adapter for a .NET object of the `DirectoryEntry` type. In developers' language, ADSI is a wrapper for the `DirectoryEntry` object that allows you to work with users and groups in a much more simple, convenient, and consistent way rather than dealing with exposing the raw object to the surface.

```
#Get [ADSI] full type name
PS C:\> [ADSI].FullName
System.DirectoryServices.DirectoryEntry
```

The following code example demonstrates how you can create an object once by using the ADSI type adapter, and once by using the `New-Object` cmdlet:

```
#using ADSI
PS C:\> $User = [ADSI]"WinNT://$env:ComputerName/Administrator"

#using New-Object cmdlet
PS C:\> $User = New-Object System.DirectoryServices.DirectoryEntry
"WinNT://$env:ComputerName/Administrator"
```

> An ADSI adapter can be used for both the domain and workgroup environments; however, it is better and recommended to use the `ActiveDirectory` module for managing the domain users and groups.

Creating a new local user account

For creating a new local user account, follow the given steps:

1. The first step before you create a local user account is to connect to the computer where you want to create this account. This computer could be a local or remote computer.

   ```
   #Connect to computer
   $Server = [ADSI]"WinNT://SHERIFT-Win8"
   ```

2. Then, invoke the `Create()` method to create a new account by specifying the type of object (for example, a user or group) and its name.

   ```
   #Create user object
   $User = $Server.Create("User","Test")
   ```

3. Next, set a password for this new account by invoking the `SetPassword()` method.

   ```
   #Set User Password
   $User.SetPassword("P@ssw0rd")
   ```

4. Finally, commit the changes and create the user by invoking the `CommitChanges()` method.

   ```
   #Commit Changes
   $User.CommitChanges()
   ```

Modifying an existing local user account

This task demonstrates how to use an ADSI type adapter to read and modify attributes for an existing user account:

1. First off, you have to get the user to modify attributes in the same way as you want to connect to a computer.

   ```
   #retrieving an existing user "Test"
   $User = [ADSI]"WinNT://SHERIFT-CoEx/Test,User"
   ```

2. Then, you can manipulate this `$User` object to either get or set an existing user attribute.

   ```
   #Set user attributes
   $User.FullName = "Test Account01"
   $User.Description = "A Test User for application testers"
   ```

3. Finally, commit the changes and create an update of the user by invoking the `CommitChanges()` method.

   ```
   #Commit Changes
   $User.CommitChanges()
   ```

Adding and removing a user account to and from a group

In order to add or remove a user to or from a group, you have to first get the user you want to change, and also the group you want to add or remove the user from.

```
#retrieving an existing user "Test"
$TestUser = [ADSI]"WinNT://SHERIFT-CoEx/Test,User"
#retrieving an existing group "Administrators"
$AdminsGroups = [ADSI]"WinNT://SHERIFT-CoEx/Administrators,Group"
```

Now, add the Test user to the Administrators group using the Add() method, or remove it using the Remove() method.

```
#Add user "Test" to group "Administrators"
$AdminsGroups.Add($TestUser.Path)
#Remove user "Test" from group "Administrators"
$AdminsGroups.Remove($TestUser.Path)
```

Removing an existing local user account

Removing an existing user account or group is similar to the creation process; however, you need to invoke the Delete() method instead of the Create() method.

```
#Connect to computer
$Server = [ADSI]"WinNT://SHERIFT-Win8"
#retrieving an existing user "Test"
$TestUser = [ADSI]"WinNT://SHERIFT-Win8/Test,User"
#Remove user object
$Server.Delete('User',$TestUser.Name.Value)
```

> The same method applies when you want to remove an existing group.

Listing all the existing users and groups

Local users and groups can be retrieved by calling the computer's children. The computer's children contain the list of all users, groups, and services on this computer, so you can filter the list by the type of classes and select only the classes of users and groups.

```
#Connect to computer
$Server = [ADSI]"WinNT://SHERIFT-Win8"
#Get computer's children
$Server.Children | Group Class | Select Count,Name
Count Name
----- ----
    3 User
   19 Group
  205 Service
#Filter children by class type
$Server.Children | Where {$_.Class -eq "User" -or $_.Class -eq
"Group"} | Select Name,SchemaClassName
Name                                       SchemaClassName
----                                       ---------------
{Administrator}                            User
```

```
{Guest}                                User
{Test}                                 User
{UpdatusUser}                          User
{Access Control Assistance Operators}  Group
{Administrators}                       Group
{Backup Operators}                     Group
{Cryptographic Operators}              Group
{Distributed COM Users}                Group
(...)
```

Managing web servers – IIS

IIS provides a set of cmdlets that allows you to easily manage, configure, and operate your Windows web servers. These cmdlets are shipped in a PowerShell module called `WebAdministration`. This module can be used to deal with different components such as websites, web apps, virtual directories, application pools, and the like.

You can manually import the `WebAdministration` module into the running instance of the Windows PowerShell console session by using the `Import-Module` cmdlet as shown in the following code line:

```
PS C:\>Import-Module WebAdministration
```

Working with web application pools

Web application pools are used to group one or more websites or web applications routed to the same IIS worker process, which makes them easy to control, manage, and administer. The worker process serves as the process boundary that separates each web application pool, so whenever one worker process or application is having an issue or recycles, the other applications or worker processes are not affected.

To create a new web application pool, you have to use the `New-WebAppPool` cmdlet:

```
#Create new Web Application Pool
PS C:\>New-WebAppPool -Name myWebAppPool

Name                      State        Applications
----                      -----        ------------
myWebAppPool              Started
```

Unfortunately, the `New-WebAppPool` cmdlet creates the application pool with the default settings with no ability to modify or define new settings. However, you can still modify the application pool's settings by using the `IIS:\` provider. The following example demonstrates how you can access the pool's properties and change them via the `Get-Item` and `Set-Item` cmdlets:

```
#Get "myWebAppPool" Application Pool
$myWebAppPool = Get-Item IIS:\AppPools\myWebAppPool

#Change Managed Runtime Version from v4.0 to v2.0
$myWebAppPool.managedRuntimeVersion = "v2.0"

#Change Managed Pipeline Version from Integrated to Classic
$myWebAppPool.managedPipelineMode = "Classic"

#Enable 32-bit Applications
$myWebAppPool.enable32BitAppOnWin64 = $true

#Change the Start Mode from OnDemand to AlwaysOn
$myWebAppPool.startMode = "AlwaysOn"

#Change AppPool Identity
#Set Identity Username
$myWebAppPool.processModel.userName = "WebAppPoolUser"

#Set Identity Password
$myWebAppPool.processModel.password = "P@ssword"

#Set Identity Type custom Account "3"
$myWebAppPool.processModel.identityType = 3

#Commit the Changes
$myWebAppPool | Set-Item
```

Creating a new website

To create a new basic IIS website, you have to use the `New-Website` cmdlet combined with parameters such as `-Name`, `-Port`, `-HostHeader`, and `-ApplicationPool`. The following code demonstrates how to create a new website `myWebSite` on port 80 and as a part of the `myWebAppPool` application pool:

```
#Create new IIS website
PS C:\> New-Website -Name myWebSite -Port 80 -HostHeader myWebSite
-PhysicalPath c:\inetpub\myWebSite -ApplicationPool myWebAppPool
```

```
Name          ID   State      Physical Path      Bindings
----          --   -----      -------------      --------
myWebSite     2    Started    c:\myWebSite       http *:80:myWebSite
```

Creating a new virtual directory

IIS virtual directories can be created using the `New-WebVirtualDirectory` cmdlet. The following code demonstrates how to create a new virtual directory `mySites` under the default IIS website called `Default Web Site`:

```
#Create new Virtual Directory
PS C:\> New-WebVirtualDirectory -Site "Default Web Site" -Name
  mySites -PhysicalPath c:\inetpub\mySites
```

Creating a new web application

An IIS web application is being created exactly like a virtual directory even with the same parameters; the only difference is we use the `New-WebApplication` cmdlet instead of the `New-WebVirtualDirectory` cmdlet.

```
#Create new Web Application
PS C:\> New-WebApplication -Site "Default Web Site" -Name myWebApp
  -PhysicalPath c:\inetpub\myWebApp
```

As both the virtual directory and the web application are almost the same, you can convert any existing virtual directory to a web application using the `ConvertTo-WebApplication` cmdlet.

```
#Convert Virtual Directory to Web Application
PS C:\> ConvertTo-WebApplication 'IIS:\Sites\Default Web
  Site\mySites'

Name             Application pool   Protocols    Physical Path
----             ----------------   ---------    -------------
mySites          DefaultAppPool     http
```

Creating an FTP site

You can also work with FTP sites by using PowerShell cmdlets. You can create a new FTP site using the `New-WebFtpSite` cmdlet.

```
#Create new FTP site
PS C:\>New-WebFtpSite -Name myFTPSite -Port 21 -PhysicalPath
  c:\inetpub\FTP

Name             ID   State      Physical Path      Bindings
----             --   -----      -------------      --------
myFTPSite        3    Started    c:\inetpub\FTP     ftp *:21:
```

Make sure that you have FTP 7 or a later version installed in order to have this cmdlet work successfully.

Creating and modifying an existing website binding

Another task that you might need to do is add a new web binding to your website. The following example demonstrates how to use the `New-WebBinding` and `Set-WebBinding` cmdlets to create a new HTTPs web binding for the default IIS website, and then modify the existing HTTP binding to use another port:

```
#Create HTTPs web binding
PS C:\> New-WebBinding -Name 'Default Web Site' -Protocol Https -
  Port 443
#Change HTTP web binding port from 80 to 7288
PS C:\> Set-WebBinding -Name 'Default Web Site' -
  BindingInformation "*:80:" -PropertyName Port -Value 7288
```

Backing up and restoring the web configuration

As a developer, you make changes to your development environment all the time, either to adopt a new technology or to apply a change in your application. This means that you might do a change that corrupts the whole environment, and this is why they invented the backup, so that you can safely revert your changes and get everything up and running again in no time.

The following code sample shows how to back up and restore your IIS webserver's configuration:

```
#Backup IIS webserver configuration
PS C:\> Backup-WebConfiguration -Name myWebServerBackup

Name                                 Creation Date
----                                 -------------
myWebServerBackup                    11/4/2013 12:00:00 AM

#Restore IIS webserver configuration
PS C:\> Restore-WebConfiguration -Name myWebServerBackup
```

You can also use the `Get-WebConfigurationBackup` cmdlet to get a list of available IIS configuration back ups.

```
PS C:\> Get-WebConfigurationBackup

Name                                 Creation Date
----                                 -------------
myWebServerBackup                    11/4/2013 12:00:00 AM
```

Whenever the web configuration backup file is no longer needed, you can simply use the `Remove-WebConfigurationBackup` cmdlet with the `-Name` parameter to remove it.

SQL Server and Windows PowerShell

SQL Server provides a Windows PowerShell module called `SQLPS` that helps SQL Server DBAs, IT professionals, and developers benefit from the capabilities of Windows PowerShell to work with T-SQL and XQuery in order to perform complex SQL Server administration and automation tasks.

The SQL Server PowerShell module includes a SQL Server Provider, `SQLSERVER:\`, similar to the other PowerShell providers. This SQL Provider allows you to navigate through the component as if you are working with a filesystem, so you can use the native commands to navigate, rename, and delete objects. For instance, in case of SQL Server, you can work with server instances, databases, tables, and so on.

> For more information about the PowerShell Provider, refer to `http://msdn.microsoft.com/en-us/library/windows/desktop/ee126186(v=vs.85).aspx` and `http://technet.microsoft.com/en-us/library/hh847791.aspx`.

The following screenshot shows how easy it is to use a native command such as the `dir` command with the SQL Server provider to list the available databases as if they are files and folders:

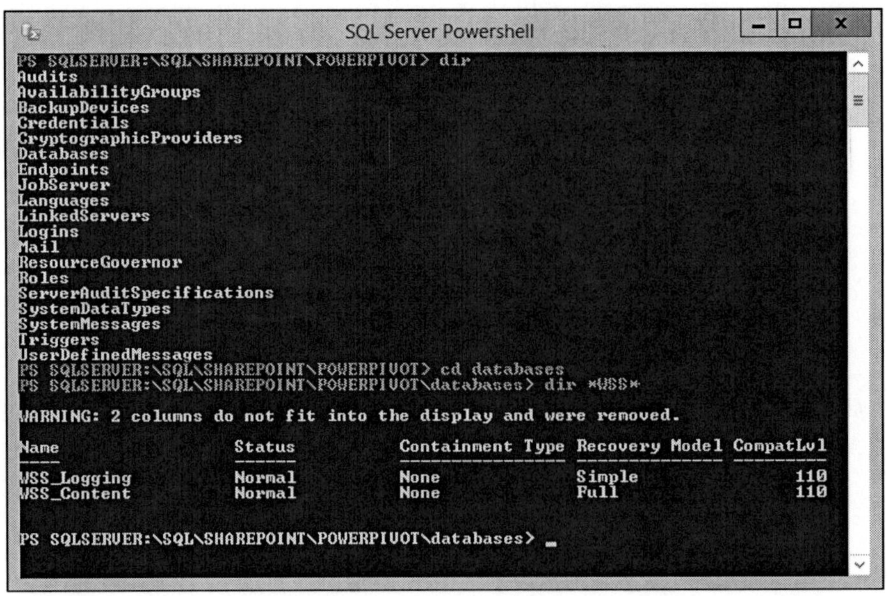

Loading SQL Server PowerShell

Loading the SQL Server PowerShell module can be done either by importing the module directly into the running instance of a PowerShell session like what we did previously with the `WebAdministration` module, or by launching it directly from the **SQL Server Management Studio** (**SSMS**) interface.

Importing SQL Server PowerShell module

The following line of code demonstrates how to load the `SQLPS` module into a running PowerShell session:

```
#Import SQL Server PowerShell Module
PS C:\> Import-Module SQLPS -DisableNameChecking
```

Launching the SQL Server PowerShell from SSMS

You can also perform the following steps to launch a SQL-aware PowerShell session directly from the SSMS:

1. Open the **Microsoft SQL Server Management Studio**.
2. Right-click on any item under the **Object Explorer** pane.

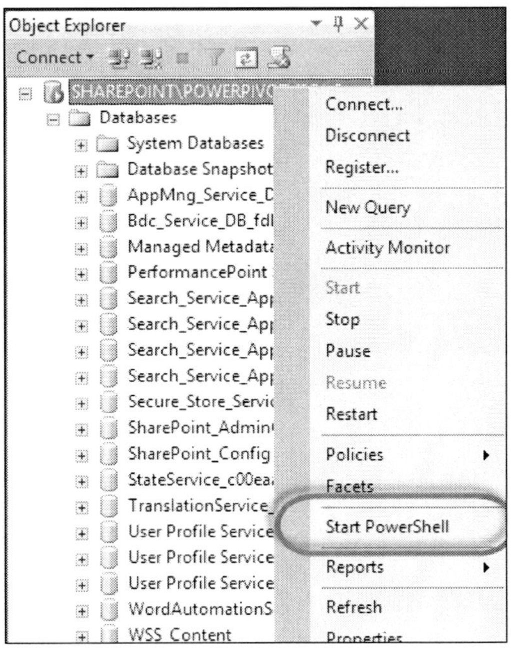

3. Select **Start PowerShell** to launch the SQL PowerShell.

Working with the SQL Server scripting

In this section, we will help you to get started with SQL Server scripting and automation by using a set of Windows PowerShell scenarios and examples.

Example 1 – executing the T-SQL statement

In this example, you want to automate a set of SQL Server tasks that require the execution of T-SQL statements via PowerShell. For this purpose, you have to use the `Invoke-Sqlcmd` cmdlet with the following group of parameters:

- `-ServerInstance`: This defines the SQL Server instance
- `-Database`: This gives the name of the database
- `-Hostname`: This gives the name of the server running the SQL Server
- `-Query`: This defines the T-SQL statement

The following code shows how to use the `Invoke-Sqlcmd` cmdlet to run a T-SQL query against the `Master` database hosted on the default SQL server instance on the server `SQL01`:

```
#Invoke SQL Query using PowerShell
PS :\> Invoke-Sqlcmd -ServerInstance SQL01\MSSQLSERVER -Database
  Master -Query "SELECT db_name(dbid) as DB,name,filename FROM
  sysaltfiles" -HostName SQL01
```

Example 2 – backing up the SQL Server database

In this example, you want to use PowerShell to back up all the SQL Server databases hosted under a specific instance. For this purpose, you have to use the `Backup-SqlDatabase` cmdlet.

The following code shows how to use the `Backup-SqlDatabase` cmdlet to back up both database files and logfiles, and then store the backup files in the `C:\Backup` directory:

```
ForEach($Database in (Get-ChildItem
  SQLSERVER:\SQL\MSSQLSERVER\Databases))
{
  $FilePath = "C:\Backup\" + $Database.Name + ".bak"
  $LogFilePath = "C:\Backup\" + $Database.Name + ".log"

  #Backup Database File
Backup-SqlDatabase -ServerInstance SQL01\MSSQLSERVER -Database
  $Database.Name -BackupAction Database -BackupFile $FilePath

#backup Database Log File
```

```
Backup-SqlDatabase -ServerInstance SQL01\MSSQLSERVER -Database
  $Database.Name -BackupAction Log -BackupFile $LogFilePath
}
```

Example 3 – restoring the SQL Server database

In this example, you want to use PowerShell to restore a SQL Server database. For this purpose, you have to use the `Restore-SqlDatabase` cmdlet.

The following code shows how to use the `Rstore-Sqlcmd` cmdlet to restore all the databases' backups stored in specific files. These backup files could be previously exported either by the `Backup-Sqlcmd` cmdlet or by directly using the backup wizard in SSMS.

```
$BackupFolder = "C:\Backup\"
$ServerInstance = "SQL01\MSSQLSERVER"

ForEach($File in (Get-ChildItem $BackupFolder))
{
   $DatabaseName = $File.Name.Replace(".bak","")
    #Restore Database File
Restore-SqlDatabase -ServerInstance $ServerInstance -Database
$DatabaseName -RestoreAction Database -BackupFile $File.FullName
}
```

Example 4 – generating the SQL script for a database, tables, and stored procedures

In this example, you want to generate a SQL script for a specific database and its tables and stored procedures. For this purpose, you can use the SQL **Server Management object** (**SMO**) in combination with PowerShell to generate the SQL scripts.

The following code shows how to use the .NET integration in PowerShell to load SQL SMO assemblies in order to extend the PowerShell capabilities while working with SQL Server. This code demonstrates the loading of the SMO assembly, creating an SMO object, and then manipulating that object to generate the SQL script as an example.

```
$ServerInstance = "SQL01\MSSQLSERVER"
$ExportFolder = "C:\SqlScripts"

#Load SQL SMO assembly
[void][System.Reflection.Assembly]::LoadWithPartialName('Microsoft
  .SqlServer.SMO')
#Create SMO object of SQL Server Instance
$Server = new-object ('Microsoft.SqlServer.Management.Smo.Server')
```

```
    $ServerInstance

#Iterate over the list of the databases under the Server Instance
ForEach($Database in $Server.Databases)
{
  #Create Folder for each Database
  New-Item -ItemType Directory -Path ("$ExportFolder\" +
    $Database.Name + "\") | Out-Null
  #Create folder for tables under each database folder
  New-Item -ItemType Directory -Path ("$ExportFolder\" +
    $Database.Name + "\Tables\") | Out-Null
  #Create folder for stored procedures under each database folder
  New-Item -ItemType Directory -Path ("$ExportFolder\" +
    $Database.Name + "\StoredProcedures\") | Out-Null

  #Generate and Export Database Script
  $Database.Script() | Out-File ("$ExportFolder\" +
    $Database.Name + "\" + $Database.Name + ".sql")

  #Iterate over the list of the tables under each database
  ForEach($table in $Database.Tables)
  {
    #Generate and Export Tables Scripts
    $table.Script() | Out-File ("$ExportFolder\" +  $Database.Name
      + "\Tables\" + $table.Name + ".sql")
  }

  #Iterate over the list of the stored procedures under each
    database
  ForEach($SP in $Database.StoredProcedures)
  {
    #Generate and Export Stored Procedures Scripts
    $SP.Script() | Out-File ("$ExportFolder\" +  $Database.Name +
      "\StoredProcedures\" + $SP.Name + ".sql")
  }
}
```

Summary

In this chapter, we have seen a part of Windows PowerShell's capabilities with Windows Server, Internet Information Services, and SQL Server, and the real value of using it to manage and administer such a complex technology. We also learned how to use PowerShell to perform different administration tasks that we might face on a daily basis, such as preparing application requirements, handling permissions of users and groups, managing and configuring IIS, maintaining SQL Server databases, and many more interesting topics.

This chapter was not intended to give you everything about the mentioned technologies; however, it intended to give you an overview and ensure that you deeply understand, as much as possible, how these technologies can work smoothly with PowerShell via a set of real scenarios and examples.

In the next chapter, we will continue the Windows PowerShell learning journey. The light will shine on unveiling the hidden power of PowerShell cmdlets to work with web technologies including, but not limited to, working with JSON, web services, RESTful applications, and social networking.

4
PowerShell and Web Technologies

Nowadays, everything is all about the Internet. In the past, we used to have the Internet just for e-mails, news, e-shopping, and few more. Although we were happy with those services, they extended very fast to have the web-based **Line of Business** (**LOB**) applications instead of the traditional desktop applications. Then, the Cloud concept was introduced, and now we can have archive and storage backup, servers and virtual machines, and even development tools on the Internet.

What really makes Internet a black horse is its mobility. You have your toolbox available anywhere anytime. In addition, you do not have to worry about compatibility issues as in the past. You will be able to use your application on any platform or device, all you need is just a web browser.

For all of these, starting with Version 3.0, Windows PowerShell became a web-aware technology with built-in support for different web technologies. You can see this in Windows PowerShell Web Access, PowerShell Web Services, and the different web cmdlets that will be covered through this chapter.

In this chapter, we will cover:

- Working with XML web services and REST APIs
- Downloading files from the Internet
- Fetching web feeds such as Atom and RSS
- Working with JSON

Web cmdlets in PowerShell

Windows PowerShell comes with a nice set of cmdlets that make interaction with the Internet easier than any other scripting language. In this section, we will learn about these cmdlets with examples.

Working with web services

Web services are XML-based application components that follow open standards such as **Simple Object Access Protocol** (**SOAP**) and **Web Services Description Language** (**WSDL**). Web services are mainly used for open communication and interoperability among different platforms over the Internet.

In PowerShell, the `New-WebServiceProxy` cmdlet creates a web service proxy object that allows you to access, utilize, and invoke XML web services directly from your PowerShell code.

Example 1 – using the GeoIPService web service

The **GeoIPService** web service allows you to look up the geographic location of an IP address. The following example demonstrates how to invoke the GeoIPService method called `GetGeoIP("<IP_ADDRESS>")`, which retrieves the geographic location for the IP address:

```
#GeoIPService URI
$Uri = 'http://www.webservicex.net/geoipservice.asmx?WSDL'

#Create new WebServiceProxy Object
$GeoIPWebService = New-WebServiceProxy -Uri $Uri -Namespace
myWebServiceProxy

#Invoke GetGeoIP("IPaddress") method
$GeoIPWebService.GetGeoIP('213.131.66.246')

ReturnCode        : 1
IP                : 213.131.66.246
ReturnCodeDetails : Success
CountryName       : Egypt
CountryCode       : EGY
```

You can use the `GetGeoIPContext()` method to get the geographic information of the IP address you are using when you are calling the web service:

```
#Invoke GetGeoIPContext() method
$GeoIPWebService.GetGeoIPContext()
```

Example 2 – using the Stock Quote web service

The **Stock Quote** web service allows you to look up the latest stock information for a specific company by its stock symbol. A **stock symbol** is a series of unique characters that represents a company in the stock market. For example, the stock symbol for Microsoft is MSFT, and Google is GOOG. The following example demonstrates how to look up Microsoft stock using the Stock Quote method called `GetQuote("STOCK_SYMBOL")`:

```
#Stock Quote URI
$Uri = 'http://www.webservicex.net/stockquote.asmx?WSDL'

#Create new WebServiceProxy Object
$StockQuote = New-WebServiceProxy -Uri $Uri -Namespace
myWebServiceProxy

#Invoke GetQuote("STOCK_SYMBOL") method
$StockQuote.GetQuote('MSFT')

<StockQuotes><Stock><Symbol>MSFT</Symbol><Last>37.841</
Last><Date>11/15/2013</Date><Time>4:00pm</Time><Change>-0.18</
Change><Open>37.95</Open><High>38.02</High><Low>37.72</
Low><Voume>50602032</Volume><MktCap>315.9B</
MktCap><PreviousClose>38.021</PreviousClose><PercentageChange>-0.47%</
PercentageChange><AnnRange>26.26-38.22</AnnRange><Earns>2.671</
Earns><P-E>14.23</P-E><Name>Microsoft Corpora</Name></Stock></
StockQuotes>
```

Unlike the GeoIPService example, the Stock Quote web service returns unstructured XML data that makes it hard to read. To get over such a problem in similar cases, we can use a trick from *Chapter 2, Unleashing Your Development Skills with PowerShell*. This trick is simply storing the unstructured XML string in a strongly typed variable of XML data type. Thus, PowerShell will automatically convert it to an XML object by casting the unstructured string to XML standard format:

```
#XML casting of $StockQuote
[XML] $Stock = $StockQuote.GetQuote('MSFT')

#Read Stock information
$Stock.StockQuotes.Stock

Symbol              : MSFT
Last                : 37.841
Date                : 11/15/2013
Time                : 4:00pm
Change              : -0.18
Open                : 37.95
Name                : Microsoft Corporation
```

Working with web requests

The `Invoke-WebRequest` cmdlet allows you to get and capture contents from a website. This cmdlet returns an `HttpWebResponseObject` object that contains all information about the web request, such as response code, response description, links, forms, and buttons. You can also think of `Invoke-WebRequest` as the PowerShell implementation of the `System.Net.HttpWebRequest` .NET class, so that you have many parameters that reflect the properties of this class, such as `ContentType`, `Method`, `Body`, `Headers`, `Certificates`, and `UserAgent`.

Let's discover this cmdlet with a few lines of code. First off, we will invoke a request to fetch the content of a website:

```
PS C:\> $web = Invoke-WebRequest http://blogs.msdn.com/b/powershell
```

Now, we have the response stored in the `$web` variable, so we are ready to get its content and then go deeper into its other members:

```
#getting the BaseResponse of the web request
PS C:\> $web.BaseResponse
IsMutuallyAuthenticated : False
Cookies                 : {AuthorizationCookie=d114cf6b-a8d3-4af4-
869b-742773394143}
Headers                 : {Pragma, X-FRAME-OPTIONS, Telligent-
Evolution, X-Server...}
SupportsHeaders         : True
ContentLength           : 165002
ContentType             : text/html; charset=utf-8
CharacterSet            : utf-8
Server                  : Microsoft-IIS/7.5
LastModified            : 11/28/2013 5:18:09 AM
StatusCode              : OK
StatusDescription       : OK
ProtocolVersion         : 1.1
ResponseUri             : http://blogs.msdn.com/b/powershell/
Method                  : GET
IsFromCache             : False
```

You can also get the information about cookies generated by this web request, by using the following code:

```
PS C:\> $web.BaseResponse.Cookies

HttpOnly   : False
Discard    : False
Domain     : blogs.msdn.com
```

```
Expired     : False
Expires     : 1/1/0001 12:00:00 AM
Name        : AuthorizationCookie
Path        : /
Secure      : False
TimeStamp   : 11/28/2013 5:06:37 AM
Value       : d114cf6b-a8d3-4af4-869b-742773394143
```

In addition, you can also discover the forms, links, and images available on the request URI, by using the following code:

```
#Get Forms
PS C:\> $web.Forms | Format-List
Id     : aspnetForm
Method : post
Action : /b/powershell/
Fields : {[SearchTextBox_Header, Search MSDN with Bing],
[SearchTextBox_AllBlogs, Search MSDN with Bing], [SearchButton_
AllBlogs, ]...}

#Get images
PS C:\> $web.Images | Select -Property src

src
---
/themes/MSDN2/images/MSDN/logo_msdn.png
http://www.microsofttranslator.com/static/193864/img/wgshare.gif
/Utility/images/small-stars/star-left-on.png
/Utility/images/small-stars/star-right-on.png (...)

#Get links
PS C:\> $web.Links | Select -Property innerText,href

innerText                href
---------                ----
Server & Tools Blogs     http://blogs.technet.com/b/serverandtools/
Windows Server           http://blogs.technet.com/b/windowsserver/
Server & Cloud           http://blogs.technet.com/b/server-cloud/
(...)
```

This is not everything; you can still get more and more out of this response. To check out the rest of the available properties, do not forget to use the `Get-Member` cmdlet:

```
PS C:\> $web | Get-Member
```

Example 1 – downloading files from the Internet

In this example, we will compare how PowerShell was dealing with the Web before and after Version 3.0. The following code sample demonstrates the old way to download files in PowerShell. In the versions of PowerShell before the `Invoke-WebRequest` cmdlet, the files were downloaded in PowerShell using the `System.Net.WebClient` .NET framework class:

```
#The Uri for the file
$FileUri = "http://bit.ly/1aQmc4A"

#The local path to save the downloaded file
$destination = "c:\Downloads\WMF4.msu"

#Creating a System.Net.WebClient  object of System.Net.WebClient
#class
$wc = New-Object System.Net.WebClient

#Calling DownloodFile() method
$wc.DownloadFile($FileUri, $destination)
```

Although this method was not the best way, it was enough at that time. One of the drawbacks of using the preceding code is that you will not notice the progress of the download. You will find the console in busy mode executing script and will never know what is happening until it finishes executing.

Luckily, we now have the `Invoke-WebRequest` cmdlet that's made our life much easier. The following code demonstrates the same procedure followed in the preceding sample:

```
#Invoke Http request to download file
Invoke-WebRequest -Uri $FileUri -OutFile $destination
```

The nice thing about using `Invoke-WebRequest` to download files is that you will get a progress bar showing the request—download in this case—status, as shown in the following screenshot:

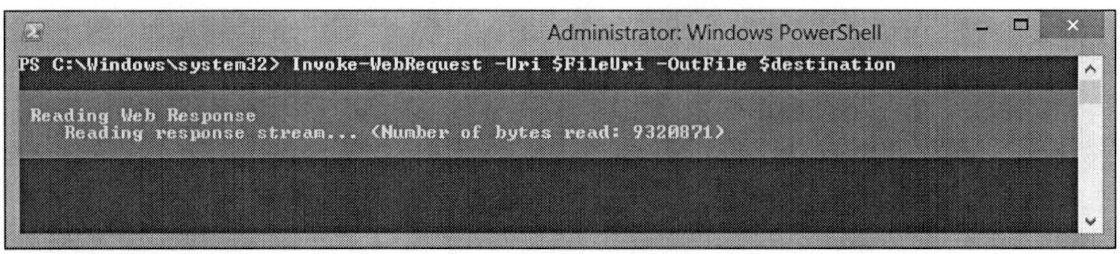

Using REST APIs

PowerShell also supports working with web services based on **REpresentational State Transfer** (**REST**) via the `Invoke-RestMethod` cmdlet. This cmdlet is similar to the `Invoke-WebRequest` cmdlet. However, it is used mainly to call any REST-based APIs and it can return either XML or JSON.

Example 1 – finding YouTube videos using PowerShell

This example will demonstrate how to perform a search in YouTube using the `Invoke-RestMethod` cmdlet along with YouTube APIs.

In order to perform a simple search using the YouTube API, you have to define at least two parameters. These parameters are the `q=` value that defines the search terms and the `v=` value that specifies the REST API version, as shown in the following snippet:

```
#Define the Youtube Search Uri
$Uri = "https://gdata.youtube.com/feeds/api/videos?v=2"

#define the search parameter and value
$Query = "&q=" + "Packt+Publishing"

#Invoke the search query
Invoke-RestMethod "$Uri$Query"
etag          : W/"D0MMRn47eCp7I2A9WhBaFUs."
id            : tag:youtube.com,2008:video:NrOzIRHLvCU
published     : 2012-09-03T14:45:46.000Z
updated       : 2013-05-26T10:51:27.000Z
category      : {category, category}
title         : Packt Publishing introduction
content       : content
link          : {link, link, link, link...}
author        : author
comments      : comments
group         : group
rating        : {gd:rating, yt:rating}
statistics    : statistics
(. . .)
```

For more information on YouTube API Query Parameters, visit https://developers.google.com/youtube/2.0/developers_guide_protocol_api_query_parameters.

Now, we have a lot of unwanted items per result. Let's filter the results by selecting a few properties such as title, link, author, and category:

```
#Invoke the search query
Invoke-RestMethod "$Uri$Query" | Select Title,Link,Author,Category
title                link           author     category
-----                ----           ------     --------
Packt Publishing     {link, link}   author     {category, category}
The Packt Web...     {link, link}   author     {category, category}
Packt celebrates... {link, link}   author     {category, category}
(...)
```

So far, the code is doing well, but unfortunately the result is not as expected. The result returned by the script is very difficult to read. So, let's add some PowerShell spices to change what results should look like. For this purpose, we will use the `PSCustomObject` type adapter. The `PSCustomObject` type adapter allows the creation of a PowerShell custom object from hash tables, so you can mix and match the results from different objects in one custom object.

```
Invoke-RestMethod "$Uri$Query"| ForEach-Object{
    [PSCustomObject]@{
        Title = $_.Title
        Author = $_.Author.name
        URL = $_.content.src
        Term = $_.category.term[1]
    }
} | format-list

Title    : Packt Publishing introduction
Author   : PacktPublishing
Link     : https://www.youtube.com/v/NrOzIRHLvCU?version=3&f=videos&ap
p=youtube_gdata
Category : Education

Title    : Applied Architecture Patterns on the Microsoft Platform
Author   : Stephen Thomas
Link     : https://www.youtube.com/v/AmZx_Gcc8DA?version=3&f=videos&ap
p=youtube_gdata
Category : Tech
(...)
```

Finally, we have the result filtered and readable, so it can be displayed in a grid using the `Out-GridView` cmdlet, or even be exported using one of the `Export-*` cmdlets.

Example 2 – reading web feeds

One of the interesting things about the `Invoke-RestMethod` cmdlet is the ability to understand the ATOM and RSS feed structure without any conversion because they are XML based. The following example demonstrates how to use `Invoke-RestMethod` to get the latest blog posts from the PowerShell team blog:

```
#Reading feeds from PowerShell team blog
$feeds = Invoke-RestMethod http://blogs.msdn.com/b/powershell/atom.
aspx

#Filtering and Formatting results
$feeds | ForEach {
    [PSCustomObject]@{
        Title=$_.title;
        Author=$_.author.name;
        Link=$_.link.href;
        Date=[DateTime]$_.published
    }
} | Format-List

Title  : Push and Pull Configuration Modes
Author : PowerShell Team
Link   : http://blogs.msdn.com/b/powershell/archive/2013/11/26/push-
and-pull-configuration-modes.aspx
Date   : 11/26/2013 9:31:25 PM

Title  : PowerShell DSC Resource for configuring Pull Server
environment
Author : PowerShell Team
Link   : {http://blogs.msdn.com/b/powershell/archive/2013/11/21/
powershell-dsc-resource-for-configuring-pull-server-environment.aspx}
Date   : 11/21/2013 8:38:00 PM
(...)
```

The same will work fine with RSS feeds. You only have to change the ATOM feed address to the RSS feed address, which is `http://blogs.msdn.com/b/powershell/rss.aspx` in our case.

Working with JSON

Java Script Object Notation (JSON) is a text-based open standard language used as an alternative to XML in order to transmit the structured data between servers and web applications in a human-readable format. Windows PowerShell introduced a couple of cmdlets that allow objects' conversion from JSON and vice versa.

Example 1 – converting objects into the JSON format

The following example demonstrates how to use the `ConvertTo-Json` cmdlet to convert a PowerShell object data to JSON. In this example, we will convert the ATOM feeds from the previous example to JSON format:

```
#Reading feeds from PowerShell team blog
$feeds = Invoke-RestMethod http://blogs.msdn.com/b/powershell/atom.
aspx

#Filtering and Formatting results
$feeds | ForEach {
     [PSCustomObject]@{
         Title=$_.title;
         Author=$_.author.name;
         Link=$_.link.href;
         Date=[DateTime]$_.published
      }
} | ConvertTo-Json
[
     {
         "Title":  "Push and Pull Configuration Modes",
         "Author":  "PowerShell Team",
         "Link":  "http://blogs.msdn.com/b/powershell/
archive/2013/11/26/push-and-pull-configuration-modes.aspx",
         "Date":  "2013-11-26T19:31:25Z"
     },
     {
         "Title":  "Resource Designer Tool - A walkthrough writing a
DSC resource",
         "Author":  "PowerShell Team",
         "Link":  "http://blogs.msdn.com/b/powershell/
archive/2013/11/19/resource-designer-tool-a-walkthrough-writing-a-dsc-
resource.aspx",
         "Date":  "2013-11-19T22:56:56Z"
     }
]
```

Example 2 – converting objects from JSON to the PowerShell format

Today, most of the web services and REST APIs return their results in JSON format. The most popular examples are social networks such as Facebook and Twitter.

Windows PowerShell also has the `ConvertFrom-Json` cmdlet that allows the conversion of an object from JSON to an object that can be manipulated as any other PowerShell object so that it can be displayed or exported to a file.

The following example demonstrates how to convert JSON to a PowerShell object using the `ConvertFrom-Json` cmdlet:

```
#JSON formatted string
$JSON =  @"
[
    {
        "Title":  "Push and Pull Configuration Modes",
        "Author":  "PowerShell Team",
        "Link":  "http://blogs.msdn.com/b/powershell/
archive/2013/11/26/push-and-pull-configuration-modes.aspx",
        "Date":  "2013-11-26T19:31:25Z"
    },
    {
        "Title":  "Resource Designer Tool - A walkthrough writing a
DSC resource",
        "Author":  "PowerShell Team",
        "Link":  "http://blogs.msdn.com/b/powershell/
archive/2013/11/19/resource-designer-tool-a-walkthrough-writing-a-dsc-
resource.aspx",
        "Date":  "2013-11-19T22:56:56Z"
    }
]
"@
#Convert JSON string to PowerShell Object
$JSON | ConvertFrom-Json
Title  : Push and Pull Configuration Modes
Author : PowerShell Team
Link   : http://blogs.msdn.com/b/powershell/archive/2013/11/26/push-
and-pull-configuration-modes.aspx
Date   : 2013-11-26T19:31:25Z

Title  : Resource Designer Tool - A walkthrough writing a DSC resource
Author : PowerShell Team
Link   : http://blogs.msdn.com/b/powershell/archive/2013/11/19/
resource-designer-tool-a-walkthrough-writing-a-dsc-resource.aspx
Date   : 2013-11-19T22:56:56Z
```

In this code, you will notice that we used the `@` symbol to define the JSON-formatted string. This type of string is called **Here-String**. The Here-String is the PowerShell mechanism to specify a block of string literals. It preserves whitespaces, line breaks, and single and double quotes. The PowerShell Here-String is similar to C# verbatim strings.

The Here-String is defined by the `@"` symbol in the first line, the `"@` symbol in the last line, and string content between both lines.

Summary

In this chapter, we have covered examples of the integration between Windows PowerShell and the Internet represented in web-related technologies such as web services and REST APIs. We also learned how to download files from the Internet and read web feeds such Atom and RSS. Moreover, we touched on working with JSON and how to covert a JSON-formatted string to PowerShell objects and vice versa.

In the next chapter, we will reach the destination of our PowerShell journey. The focus will be on the automation of the **Microsoft Application Lifecycle Management** (**ALM**) tool known as **Visual Studio Team Foundation Server** (**TFS**). We will understand how PowerShell is powerful even with pure development tools.

5

PowerShell and Team Foundation Server

Visual Studio **Team Foundation Server** (**TFS**) is a Microsoft solution that provides an end-to-end software development process, which is also known as **Application Lifecycle Management** (**ALM**). TFS provides many features, including but not limited to project management, build processes, lab deployment capabilities, reporting, automated testing, and release management and control.

Like other server products, TFS had adopted PowerShell, and now it provides PowerShell cmdlets for automating different version-control tasks. However, the provided cmdlets are not many compared to the other products, but it is still a good start and also an indication of the shiny future of PowerShell with such a development tool.

In this chapter, we will cover:

- What is TFS Power Tools
- Installing and configuring TFS PowerShell snap-in
- Working with TFS PowerShell cmdlets

TFS Power Tools

TFS Power Tools is a set of tools and command-line utilities that enhance and fine-tune the TFS. Also, it adds some extra features that increase the productivity of TFS and its users. One of these tools is Windows PowerShell cmdlets. For TFS, PowerShell cmdlets provide commands to support automation and enable scripting for basic version-control operations. In addition to PowerShell cmdlets, Power Tools includes but is not limited to Best Practice Analyzer, Windows shell extensions, and TF command lines.

TFS Power Tools is available as a separate component apart from TFS. It can be freely downloaded from the **Visual Studio Gallery** on **Microsoft Developers Network (MSDN)**.

> Visual Studio Team Foundation Server 2013 Power Tools can be found at `http://visualstudiogallery.msdn.microsoft.com/f017b10c-02b4-4d6d-9845-58a06545627f`.
>
> Visual Studio Team Foundation Server 2012 Power Tools can be found at `http://visualstudiogallery.msdn.microsoft.com/b1ef7eb2-e084-4cb8-9bc7-06c3bad9148f`.

The installation process of TFS Power Tools is very simple, and it is a straightforward wizard. Unfortunately, PowerShell cmdlets are not selected by default during the installation using the default setup settings of Power Tools. So, make sure that you are selecting the **Custom** setup option as shown in the following screenshot:

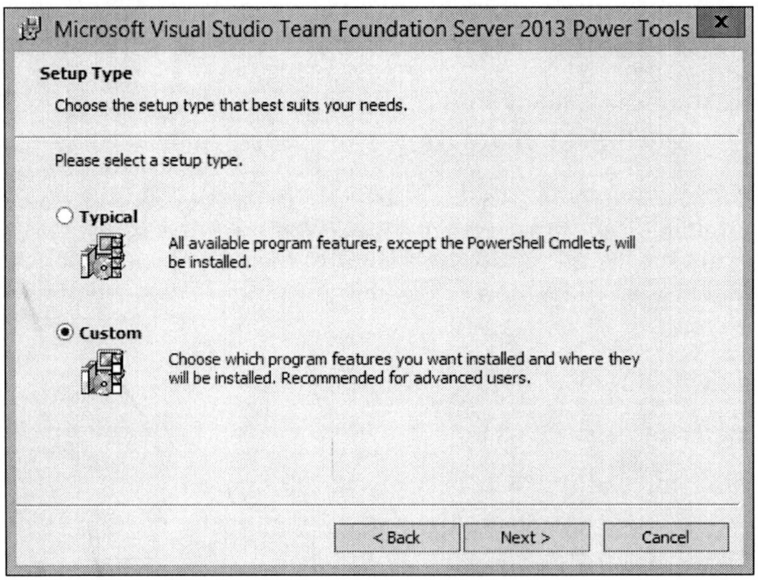

As usual, a **Custom** setup allows you to select the features that need to be installed, instead of following the default or typical setup. So, make sure that you mark the **PowerShell Cmdlets** feature for installation, as shown in the following screenshot:

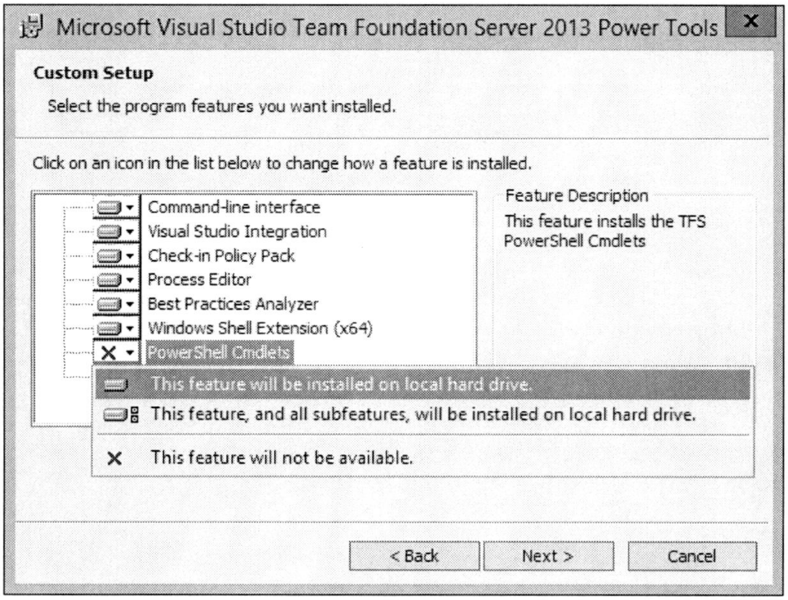

Getting started with TFS PowerShell cmdlets

Once the TFS Power Tools' installation is complete, you will find that a new PowerShell snap-in `Microsoft.TeamFoundation.PowerShell` has been registered successfully on your system. This snap-in contains the PowerShell cmdlets for TFS.

If you do not know about PowerShell snap-ins, a **Windows PowerShell snap-in** is a mechanism for registering sets of cmdlets and providers with the shell, thus extending the functionality of the shell. A PowerShell snap-in can register all the cmdlets and providers in a single assembly, or it can register a specific list of cmdlets and providers.

A PowerShell snap-in is pretty much similar to modules; to be specific, it is similar to binary modules. However, the snap-in mechanism is being deprecated and may be come out of support in future releases of PowerShell. The reason for this is that modules provide a superset of functionalities in terms of loading, distributing, and packaging cmdlets and providers.

PowerShell has cmdlets that allow you to get, add, and remove snap-ins exactly like the cmdlets for modules. Thus, you can load the TFS PowerShell snap-in using some of these cmdlets, as shown in the following example:

```
#getting snap-in information
PS C:\ > Get-PSSnapin -Registered *TeamFoundation*
Name        : Microsoft.TeamFoundation.PowerShell
PSVersion   : 3.0
Description : This is a PowerShell snap-in that includes the Team
Foundation Server cmdlets.

#loading TFS snap-in
PS C:\ > Add-PSSnapin Microsoft.TeamFoundation.PowerShell
```

Now, we have the TFS snap-in loaded to the PowerShell session and ready to use. This snap-in contains set of cmdlets to work with different features of TFS such as changesets, shelvesets, workspaces, and more. The following code retrieves the list of available cmdlets, and also the number of cmdlets for each TFS features:

```
PS C:\> Get-Command -Module Microsoft.TeamFoundation.PowerShell |
Group Noun -NoElement | Sort Count -Desc

Count Name
----- ----
    4 TfsShelveset
    3 TfsChangeset
    3 TfsPendingChange
    2 TfsWorkspace
    1 TfsServer
    1 TfsItem
    1 TfsItemProperty
    1 FixedPath
    1 FixedByte
    1 TfsItemHistory
    1 TfsChildItem
```

Moreover, Power Tools provides a PowerShell script `TFSSnapin.ps1` that creates PowerShell aliases for the TFS cmdlets. These aliases map the PowerShell cmdlets to the legacy commands in `tf.exe`, which is also known as **TF Command-Line Utility**. For example, there is an alias `tfserver` for the `Get-TfsServer` cmdlet, and an alias `tfworkspace` for the `Get-TfsWorkspace` cmdlet. This mapping is intending to make it easier for the developers who already have experience with this command-line utility.

> The `TFSSnapin.ps1` script is located under **Program Files (x86)** | **Microsoft Team Foundation Server 2013 Power Tools**.

Working with TFS PowerShell cmdlets

Unfortunately, the help resources and documentation for the TFS PowerShell cmdlets are very limited. The only available document is the Power Tools help, which covers the basic help information with almost no examples. Even using the `Get-Help` cmdlet will return nothing valuable. So, in this section, we will learn about the TFS cmdlets, understand their functionality, and also see some examples that show how to use these cmdlets.

- The PowerShell scripts in this section are created based on the TFS sample projects, which are a part of the Visual Studio ALM virtual machine created by *Brian Keller*, the Principal Technical Evangelist at Microsoft. The VSALM virtual machine is available for public download from `http://aka.ms/ALMVMs`.
- All the examples in this chapter have been tested only on TFS 2013 and Power Tools 2013. However, they should work with TFS 2012 and Power Tools 2012 as well because there are no major changes between PowerShell cmdlets in both versions except for fixing some bugs.

Retrieving TFS information

The first cmdlet to start with is `Get-TfsServer`. This cmdlet is important because TFS is a required parameter in almost every TFS PowerShell cmdlet. The function of this cmdlet is very obvious from its name. This cmdlet is being used to retrieve and display the TFS information.

The following code sample demonstrates how to use the `Get-TfsServer` cmdlet to retrieve the information of the TFS named `VSALM`:

```
#retrieve TFS
PS C:\> $tfs = Get-TfsServer http://VSALM:8080/tfs

Name                      : http://vsalm:8080/tfs
DisplayName               : http://vsalm:8080/tfs
CatalogNode               : CatalogNode instance 48499370
ConfigurationServer       : vsalm
TeamFoundationServer      : http://vsalm:8080/tfs
InstanceId                : 8e9a1d47-220d-4faf-8457-3e30555f35c7
Uri                       : http://vsalm:8080/tfs
TimeZone                  : System.CurrentSystemTimeZone
ServerCapabilities        : Email
IsHostedServer            : False
UICulture                 : en-US
SessionId                 : aa551612-ed21-4b09-a0f0-54e0955b991d
(...)
```

This cmdlet actually returns an instance of the `TfsTeamProjectCollection` class:

```
#get type of TFS object
PS C:\> $tfs.GetType().FullName
Microsoft.TeamFoundation.Client.TfsTeamProjectCollection
```

Thus, you can also use a project URL as a parameter for `Get-TfsServer` instead of the server URL:

```
#using Project URL as parameter
PS C:\> $tfsFFC = Get-TfsServer http://VSALM:8080/tfs/
FabrikamFiberCollection
```

Working with TFS items' information

Items in TFS mainly refer to the project structure as files and folders. Thus, the PowerShell cmdlets provide a way to discover and deal with these structures. PowerShell has three main cmdlets that work with TFS items. These cmdlets are `Get-TfsChildItem`, `Get-TfsItemHistory`, and `Get-TfsItemProperty`.

The following screenshot shows a sample item structure for a TFS project:

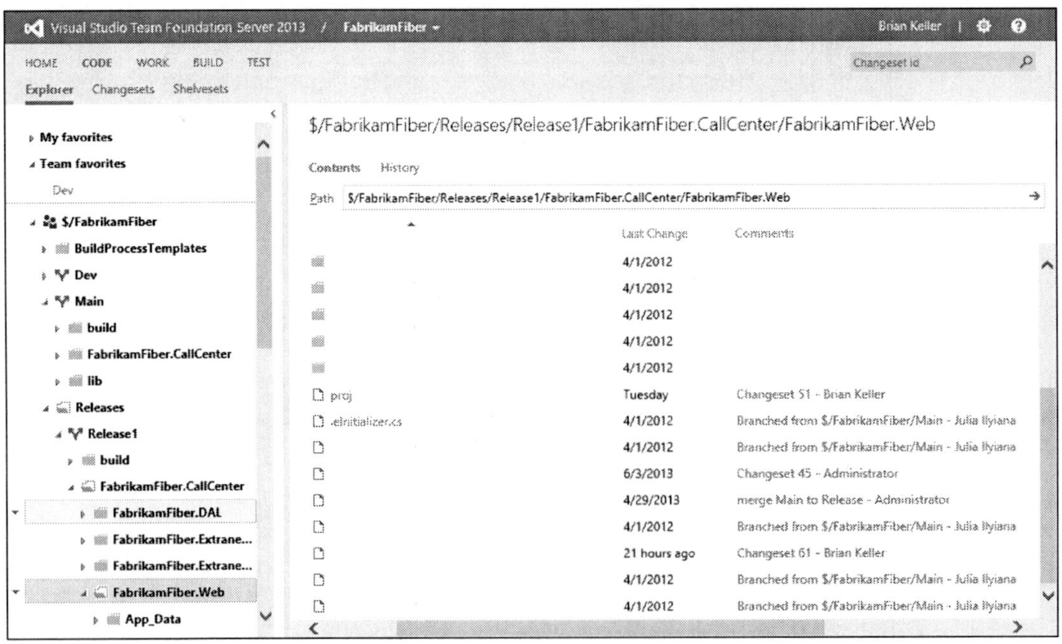

The cmdlets related to TFS items are the same as the normal items' cmdlets available in PowerShell. For example, `Get-TfsChildItem` is the same as `Get-ChildItem`, and `Get-TfsItemProperty` is the same as `Get-ItemProperty`. The benefit of using TFS cmdlets is the ability to work with the TFS project directly, but with normal item cmdlets you have to define the physical path of the project and work with it as a normal filesystem.

The `Get-TfsChildItem` cmdlet retrieves and displays the child (nested) items for a specific item. The following code sample demonstrates how to get the child items for the `FabrikamFiber` project hosted on the `FabrikamFiberCollection` project collection `$tfsFFC`:

```
#get child items for FabrikamFiber
PS C:\> Get-TfsChildItem $/FabrikamFiber -Server $tfsFFC

ChangesetId   CheckinDate   ServerItem
-------      ----------    ----------
      2      4/1/2012      $/FabrikamFiber
      3      4/1/2012      $/FabrikamFiber/BuildProcessTemplates
      7      4/1/2012      $/FabrikamFiber/Dev
      5      4/1/2012      $/FabrikamFiber/Main
      8      4/1/2012      $/FabrikamFiber/Releases
```

You pipe the previous command lines to the `Format-List` cmdlet to get more information about each item. Also, you can use the following parameters with the `Get-TfsChildItem` cmdlet:

- `-Deleted`: It is used to get the child items, including the items that have been deleted already
- `-Folders`: It is used to get the child items of only the type folder
- `-Recurse`: It is used to get the child items of each folder item until it reaches the last folder's node
- `-Version`: It is used to get the child items according to a specific criteria, such as a changeset ID or date and time

The `Get-TfsItemHistory` cmdlet retrieves and displays the history of modifications that have been made on one specific item. The following code sample demonstrates how to get the item history of the `FabrikamFiber.CallCenter.sln` item:

```
#get item history for FabrikamFiber CallCenter solution file
PS C:\>$tfsItem= "$/FabrikamFiber/Main/FabrikamFiber.CallCenter/
FabrikamFiber.CallCenter.sln"

PS C:\> Get-TfsItemHistory $tfsItem -Server $tfsFFC
```

```
Change    Owner                       CreationDate    Comment
setId
-------    -----                     ----------    -------
      63    VSALM\Brian                7/10/2013
      60    VSALM\Brian                 7/9/2013
      55    VSALM\Brian                 7/9/2013    merge Dev to Main
      29    VSALM\Administrator        4/29/2013    merge Dev to Main
      19    VSALM\Adam:1               5/16/2012
       6    VSALM\Julia:1               4/1/2012
```

In addition to the `-Version` parameter, you can also use `-User` to get the change made by a specific user, and `-Stopafter` to show a specific number of history records:

```
#get item history by user
PS C:\> Get-TfsItemHistory $tfsItem -Server $tfsFFC -User Brian

Change    Owner                       CreationDate    Comment
setId
-------    -----                     ----------    -------
      63    VSALM\Brian                7/10/2013
      60    VSALM\Brian                 7/9/2013
      55    VSALM\Brian                 7/9/2013    merge Dev to Main

#get specific number of history records
PS C:\> Get-TfsItemHistory $tfsItem -Server $tfsFFC -Stopafter 2

Change    Owner                       CreationDate    Comment
setId
-------    -----                     ----------    -------
      63    VSALM\Brian                7/10/2013
      60    VSALM\Brian                 7/9/2013
```

The last cmdlet in this group is `Get-TfsItemProperty`. This cmdlet retrieves and displays the item information such as type, item ID, path, lock status, and lock owner.

The following code sample demonstrates how to get the item properties and information using the `Get-TfsItemProperty` cmdlet:

```
#get item properties and information
PS C:\> Get-TfsItemProperty $tfsItem -Server $tfsFFC
IsInWorkspace          : False
IsLatest               : False
ChangeType             : None
PropertyValues         : {}
```

```
CheckinDate               : 7/10/2013 12:03:48 PM
DeletionId                : 0
Encoding                  : 65001
HasOtherPendingChange     : False
IsBranch                  : False
ItemId                    : 1812
ItemType                  : File
LockOwner                 : VSALM\Annie
LockOwnerDisplayName      : Annie Herriman
LockStatus                : Checkin
SourceServerItem          : $/FabrikamFiber/Main/FabrikamFiber.CallCenter/
HTMLPage2.html
TargetServerItem          : $/FabrikamFiber/Main/FabrikamFiber.CallCenter/
HTMLPage2.html
VersionLatest             : 64
VersionLocal              : 0
```

Managing TFS workspace

A workspace for Visual Studio TFS comprises of a set of working folder mappings. These mappings represent the location of client-side folders on a local disk and the corresponding repository folders on the version-control server. In addition, the name of the workspace owner and the name of the computer on which the workspace is used are also stored in TFS.

TFS PowerShell provides two cmdlets related to a TFS workspace. These cmdlets are `Get-TfsWorkspace` and `Update-TfsWorkspace`.

The `Get-TfsWorkspace` cmdlet retrieves and displays information about the currently available workspaces. The following code sample demonstrates how to get a list of workspaces for a specific project collection:

```
#get workspace information
PS C:\> Get-TfsWorkspace -Server $tfsFFC

Name                   Computer                   OwnerName
----                   --------                   ---------
VSALM                  VSALM1                      VSALM\Brian
VSALM                  VSALM2                      VSALM\Annie
```

You can also define different parameters such as `-Name`, `-Computer`, or `-Owner` to filter the results:

```
#get workspace information by owner name
PS C:\> Get-TfsWorkspace -Server $tfsFFC -Owner Brian
```

```
Name                 Computer                   OwnerName
----                 --------                   ---------
VSALM                VSALM                      VSALM\Brian
```

The second cmdlet is `Update-TfsWorkspace`. This cmdlet retrieves a copy of files from the TFS version-control server and saves it on the local workspace folder. In other words, it is used to update the workspace by either getting new files or replacing existing files. You can specify single or multiple items, overwrite existing files, and retrieve files based on the versioning criteria.

The following code sample demonstrates a very simple TFS workspace update:

```
#update TFS workspace
PS C:\ > Update-TfsWorkspace
Status      Version TargetLocalItem
------      ------- ---------------
Getting          52 C:\Users\Administrator\Source\Workspaces\
FabrikamF....
Replacing        53 C:\Users\Administrator\Source\Workspaces\
FabrikamF....
Deleting         53 $/FabrikamFiber/Dev/build/xunit.runner.visu...
```

Managing changesets, shelvesets, and pending changes

The last group of cmdlets is that of the TFS cmdlets for working and managing the TFS version-control features, such as pending changes, changesets, and shelvesets.

> You can read more about the TFS version-control features on MSDN.
>
> More information about pending changes can be found at `http://msdn.microsoft.com/en-us/library/ms181409(v=vs.100).aspx`.
>
> More information about changesets can be found at `http://msdn.microsoft.com/en-us/library/ms181408(v=vs.120).aspx`.
>
> More information about shelvesets can be found at `http://msdn.microsoft.com/en-us/library/ms245465(v=vs.100).aspx`.

The following code demonstrates how to use the `Add-TfsPendingChange` cmdlet to upload (add) a file from a local disk (workspace) to the version-control server. The parameter `-Add` is for check-in and `-Edit` is for check-out.

```
PS C:\ > $tfsItem = "C:\Users\Brian\Source\Workspaces\FabrikamFiber\
Main\FabrikamFiber.CallCenter\contactUs.html"
```

```
#add new TFS Pending change
PS C:\> Add-TfsPendingChange -Item $tfsItem -Add
Version CreationDate ChangeType      ServerItem
------- ----------   ----------      ----------
      0   7/10/2013  Add      $/Fabr..../contactUs.html
```

Another code sample demonstrates how to work with changeset cmdlets to create a new TFS changeset for the file uploaded in the previous example. It also retrieves the information of the changeset and finally updates the information of a changeset. There is no cmdlet to remove changesets because a changeset cannot be removed even from the GUI.

```
#create new TFS changeset
PS C:\> New-TfsChangeset -Item $tfsItem -Comment "my first checkin"

#Get changeset information but changeset number
PS C:\> Get-TfsChangeset -ChangesetNumber 65 -Server $tfsFFC

ChangesetId Owner           CreationDate   Comment
------- -----               ----------   -------
     65 VSALM\Brian         7/10/2013   my first checkin
#settings TFS changeset information
PS C:\> Set-TfsChangeset -Comment "checkin with comment"
-ChangesetNumber 65 -Server $tfsFFC

ChangesetId Owner           CreationDate   Comment
------- -----               ----------   -------
     65 VSALM\Brian         7/10/2013   checkin with comment
```

The following screenshot shows the changeset that has been created:

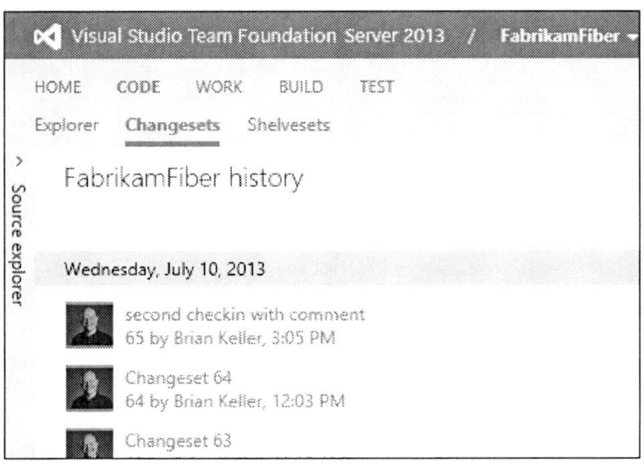

Now, we have the file that is checked in and a changeset created for it. The next demonstration is checking out this file again using the `Add-TfsPendingChange` cmdlet and then adding it on the shelve by creating a shelveset for it using the `New-TfsShelveset` cmdlet:

```
#checking out a file
PS C:\> Add-TfsPendingChange -Item $tfsItem -Edit

Version CreationDate   ChangeType      ServerItem
------- ----------   ----------      ----------
     65   1/1/0001   Edit            $/Fabri.../contactUs.html
#creating a new shelveset
PS C:\> New-TfsShelveset -Item $tfsItem -Shelveset "shelveset 1"
-Comment "my first shelveset"

Name              OwnerName      CreationDate  Comment
----              ---------       ----------   -------
shelveset 1       VSALM\Brian     7/10/2013   my first shelveset
#getting shelveset information by shelveset name
PS C:\> Get-TfsShelveset -Shelveset "shelveset 1" -Server $tfsFFC

Name            OwnerName       CreationDate   Comment
----            ---------       ----------   -------
shelveset 1     VSALM\Brian     7/10/2013   my first shelveset
```

The following screenshot shows the shelveset that has been created:

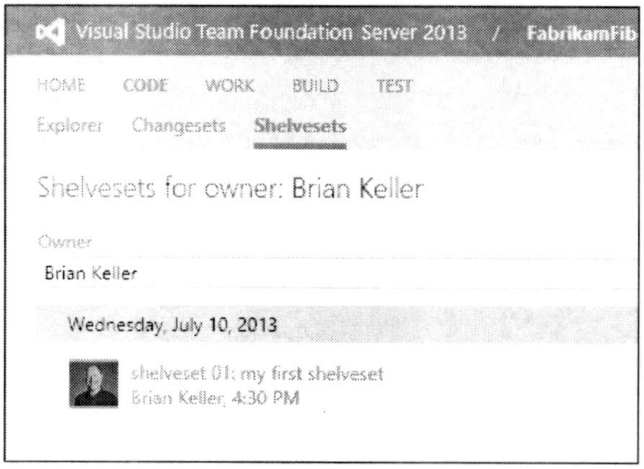

Now, you should be on a solid ground when it comes to TFS PowerShell cmdlets. We have covered almost all the TFS cmdlets. However, you might feel that you want to automate and script more features and tasks. In that case, you can use the **Team Foundation Server 2013 Object Model** along with the skills gained from *Chapter 2, Unleashing Your Development Skills with PowerShell*, of this book on how to use PowerShell with .NET objects. Thus, the sky is the limit.

> You can download the TFS 2013 Object Model using `http://visualstudiogallery.msdn.microsoft.com/3278bfa7-64a7-4a75-b0da-ec4ccb8d21b6`.
>
> Also, you can download TFS 2012 Update 4 Object Model using `http://visualstudiogallery.msdn.microsoft.com/f30e5cc7-036e-449c-a541-d522299445aa`.

Summary

In this chapter, we have learned about Team Foundation Server 2013 Power Tools, its components, and how to download and install it. We also learned about Windows PowerShell snap-in and how to load the TFS Power Tools snap-in.
Finally, we discovered with examples the TFS PowerShell cmdlets and understood their functionalities and ways to use them.

Index

D

E

F

G

H

I

R

S

X

Y

Thank you for buying

Windows PowerShell 4.0 for .NET Developers

About Packt Publishing

Packt, pronounced 'packed', published its first book "Mastering phpMyAdmin for Effective MySQL Management" in April 2004 and subsequently continued to specialize in publishing highly focused books on specific technologies and solutions.

Our books and publications share the experiences of your fellow IT professionals in adapting and customizing today's systems, applications, and frameworks. Our solution based books give you the knowledge and power to customize the software and technologies you're using to get the job done. Packt books are more specific and less general than the IT books you have seen in the past. Our unique business model allows us to bring you more focused information, giving you more of what you need to know, and less of what you don't.

Packt is a modern, yet unique publishing company, which focuses on producing quality, cutting-edge books for communities of developers, administrators, and newbies alike. For more information, please visit our website: `www.packtpub.com`.

About Packt Enterprise

In 2010, Packt launched two new brands, Packt Enterprise and Packt Open Source, in order to continue its focus on specialization. This book is part of the Packt Enterprise brand, home to books published on enterprise software - software created by major vendors, including (but not limited to) IBM, Microsoft and Oracle, often for use in other corporations. Its titles will offer information relevant to a range of users of this software, including administrators, developers, architects, and end users.

Writing for Packt

We welcome all inquiries from people who are interested in authoring. Book proposals should be sent to `author@packtpub.com`. If your book idea is still at an early stage and you would like to discuss it first before writing a formal book proposal, contact us; one of our commissioning editors will get in touch with you.

We're not just looking for published authors; if you have strong technical skills but no writing experience, our experienced editors can help you develop a writing career, or simply get some additional reward for your expertise.

[PACKT] PUBLISHING enterprise

professional expertise distilled

Instant Windows Powershell 3.0 Windows Management Instrumentation Starter

ISBN: 978-1-84968-962-5 Paperback: 66 pages

Explore new abilities of powershell 3.0 to interact with Windows Management Instrumentation (WMI) through the use of the new CIM cmdlets and realistic management scenarios

1. Learn something new in an Instant! A short, fast, focused guide delivering immediate results.
2. Create CIM sessions to local and remote systems.
3. Execute WMI queries using Windows Remote Management.

Instant Windows PowerShell

ISBN: 978-1-84968-874-1 Paperback: 54 pages

Manage and automate your Windows Server Environment efficiently using PowerShell

1. Learn something new in an Instant! A short, fast, focused guide delivering immediate results.
2. Learn to use PowerShell web access to secure Windows management anywhere, any time, on any device.
3. Understand to secure and sign the scripts you write using the script signing feature in PowerShell.

Please check **www.PacktPub.com** for information on our titles

[PACKT] enterprise
professional expertise distilled
PUBLISHING

Instant Windows PowerShell Guide

ISBN: 978-1-84968-678-5 Paperback: 86 pages

Enhance your knowledge of Windows PowerShell and get to grips with its latest features

1. Learn something new in an Instant! A short, fast, focused guide delivering immediate results.
2. Understand new CMDLETs and parameters with relevant examples.
3. Discover new module functionality such as CIM, Workflow, and DSC.
4. Acquaint yourself with enhancements to PowerShell remoting, PowerShell sessions, and desire state configuration.

Microsoft Windows PowerShell 3.0 First Look

ISBN: 978-1-84968-644-0 Paperback: 200 pages

A quick, succinct guide to the new and exciting features in PowerShell 3.0

1. Explore and experience the new features found in PowerShell 3.0.
2. Understand the changes to the language and the reasons why they were implemented.
3. Discover new cmdlets and modules available in Windows 8 and Server 8.

Please check **www.PacktPub.com** for information on our titles

CPSIA information can be obtained
at www.ICGtesting.com
Printed in the USA
FFOW02n1032250314
4477FF